DEVELOPMENT OF WESTERN EDUCATIONAL THOUGHT

About The Author

Dr. **A.P. Sharma**, born on 25 December 1932 at Dholpur, Rajasthan, India, graduated from Agra College, Agra, in the year 1954. He then shifted to Maharaja's College, Jaipur, and obtained Master's degree in English Literature in 1957. After that he served the State Education Department of Rajasthan as a Senior Master of English for almost 15 years. During this period he obtained Master's degrees in Education (1966) and Philosophy (1969) from the University of Rajasthan, Jaipur, and Ph.D. degree in Education (1972) from the University of Udaipur.

In November 1972, he was offered a senior teaching position in Nigeria where he served for more than 12 years in the Northern Universities. After relinquishing his position from the University of Sokoto in Nigeria in 1984, he joined the Catholic University at Washington D.C. for post-doctoral work. He came back to India in 1985, became Principal of R.M.V. Teachers' College at Udaipur and later Professor of Education at Vidya Bhawan Teachers' College, Udaipur. He visited Willamette University at Salem, Oragon, U.S.A. in 1990 in the capacity of a Visiting Scholar. After retiring from Vidya Bhawan in December 1991, he joined as Principal at the College of Education at Kanore, Udaipur. In 1992 he was awarded a Ph. D. degree in Philosophy from the University of Rajasthan, Jaipur. So far he has published seven books and thirty-five articles in the field of Educational Philosophy, both in India and abroad.

DEVELOPMENT OF WESTERN EDUCATIONAL THOUGHT

A.P. SHARMA
(Rtd) Professor of Education
Vidya Bhawan Teachers'
College (IASE) Udaipur.

CONCEPT PUBLISHING COMPANY, NEW DELHI - 110059

ISBN 81-7022-600-7
First Published 1997

Published and Printed by
Ashok Kumar Mittal
CONCEPT PUBLISHING COMPANY
A/15-16, Commercial Block, Mohan Garden,
NEW DELHI - 110059 (India)
Phones: 5554042, 5504042

PREFACE

One cannot doubt that History of Education is a relevant document which can transport us all the way back in the past and familiarise us with the educational thought and practice that have grown out of the different ways and patterns of human lives in the past centuries.

History of Education also provides us with some insights into the way the educational problems have been resolved in the past. Consequently it can help the professional teachers to understand educational issues and new trends which have been prominent in the past, and enlighten them to meet the challenges which would emerge before them.

It would be quite impossible to record in such a small treatise each detail of the educational growth that took place from the fourth century B.C. to the twentieth century A.D. However, efforts have been made to record all the important educational movements and trends during these centuries, including the names of the educationists whose influence on educational thought and practice have been colossal. Efforts have also been made to record the theories of education which were propounded by the educational philosophers and which were instrumental in changing the shape of education in different centuries. It is, therefore, believed that this book will be of great utility to the under-graduate and post-graduate university teachers and students of Education and all those for whom chronological knowledge of educational events, theories and practices are of immense value.

A.P. Sharma

Dedicated to
my teachers

Kr. Laloo Singh
Prof. L.K. Oad

CONTENTS

CHAPTER-I

GREEK EDUCATIONAL THOUGHTS

Ancient Greece was composed of different groups having different racial origins. These tribes, clans or 'city states', as they were called later on, seemed to have some common traditions and social and cultural goals. But the 'city states' also had sharp differences, which perhaps guided them to hostility against each other.

The principal city-states, whose influence was lasting, were Athens and Sparta which represented Ionian and Dorian cultural ideals respectively.

More than Sparta, it is Athens from where we trace the sources of the present-day cultural ideals which could be seen as the foundation of Western education. It would appear to be true that Greeks must have learned from others but they also created some models of human culture which proved ideal to the Western world. The Greeks are supposed to be the first people who seriously recognised the importance of human values and who dedicated themselves to the pursuit of art, culture and education.[1]

Before going into the details of Spartan and Athenian way of life and training, it seems necessary to have some knowledge of the Homeric period, which mainly laid the foundation of Greek education.

The Homeric Age

The Greek or Hellenic civilization began towards the end of the twelfth century B.C. The poet Homer could be ragarded as the first educator of Greeks. The aim of education was 'arete', which means 'excellence'. Homer's two famous books—the 'Illiad' and the 'Odyssey', are the two main sources which contain the early Greek educational ideals. Achilles, the hero of the Illiad, was a man of action. Odysseus, the hero of the Odyssey, contained wisdom. These two qualities combined together formed an ideal Greek person. It is worth noticing that the high expectations of 'excellence' were limited to the aristocratic class only and did not apply to the other inhabitants of the state, who were mostly foreigners and slaves.

The aim of Homeric education was to enable the leaders to set forth worthy examples which could be initiated by the youth. The brave and the wise became the models for emulation. A Greek teacher was usually an older and experienced man, who accompanied the youth to the court, the market place, the battle-field, and showed them other aspects of social life. The education of the young was ensured through teaching, personal examples and through initiation into all the activities which were practised by the older people in the club, the gymnasium and the banques.

The Homeric traditions in education influenced later Greek periods of Spartan and Athenian education. The Greece of those days was a small country with about 500,100 inhabitants. Greece comprised a small number of city-states. The most important ones were Attica with Athens as its central city, and Laconis with Sparta as its central city. In case of outside threat, a number of states got together in mutual defence, but it did not mean that they were friendly with each other all the time. They did not hesitate to make war on each other whenever their interests clashed. Because of the republican character of Greeks and because the city-states constantly were at war with each other and with their neighbours, there was a great need to develop military men who were also prudent both in war and peace.

Eventually, city-states such as Athens and Sparta united into a Greek nation, but there was little success in such attempts because of mutual jealousies. The Greek society was built on the class basis having citizens, foreigners and slaves. The foreigners and slaves were deprived of many rights which the citizens enjoyed. Perhaps suspicions about the foreigners and slaves might have also put hinderences in the way to unity of the city-states.

Nevertheless, it is worth mentioning that Greeks in general and the people of Attica in particular, were the first to attain a high degree of civilization in the Western world, specially in the area of formalized education. This played a very important role in the growth of Western civilization.

Life and Education in Sparta

Spartan citizens were a master class, ruling a majority of the people known as non-citizens. The non-citizens, mainly slaves or helots and a few foreigners, lived in the city-state.

The citizens, adult males, numbered perhaps 10,000 at the most and were themselves subdivided into social classes, headed by the landed aristocracy who dominated the government. This in turn, was based upon a popular assembly which delegated authority to a council of twenty-eight and two co-regent or kings, who functioned mainly as hereditary executives.[2]

The geographical, political and social factors existing in Lacedaemon or Sparta dictated the style and the type of education given in the country. Lacedaemon, the home of the Spartans, was surrounded by hostile states. Military preparedness was, thus, essential to the existence of Spartans. In addition to the external threat, there lurked danger within the boundary of the country. The slaves were troublesome and had to be held in check. Thus, military training was the top priority of the Spartans. Artistic and literary activities were, therefore, neglected. In fact, the Spartans treated war itself as a purely liberal art.

Aim of Education

The aim of Spartan education was to prepare citizens to safeguard the State. They were to obey the laws of the State. In short, the individual was to be trained to be loyal to his country. The young ones were the property of the State. Severe punishment, disgrace, social boycott or even death awaited them if they failed in their duties to the State.

Education of Men

The Spartans realised that to turn out a brave and loyal citizen was quite a difficult task. Therefore, the state exercised complete control over education. The process of education started after the birth of a male child. The child was examined by a council of elders appointed by the state. If the child was found to be a weakling, he was taken to Mount Taugetos and exposed to death or was rescued by helots.[3] But if he was approved by the council, he was left to the care of his parents. The mother looked after the boy up to the age of seven. She cared for a girl a little longer. The early years of the boy were spent in preparation for life away from home; that is, he became physically and psychologically ready to live away from his family.

In the eighth year, the boy was taken away to live with boys of his age in the barracks. The boys were organised into 'packs' or 'companies'. They were exposed to harsh routine of life and did running, boxing, wrestling and military drills. They received instructions in Spartan manners and virtues. Such manners were stern and unbending. The food and clothing were inadequate, so the boys went barefooted and on hard beds. It is from such ordeals that the expression 'Spartan life', meaning hard life has come down to us.

The principal teacher of the boys was a citizen of rank and a soldier of repute. He had a number of assistants who obeyed him and discharged specific duties. Any older citizen could be the teacher as all had passed through the rigor of training, but special appointments were also made.

The boys stayed and trained in the barracks up to the age of eighteen years. Then they became cadets. For the next two years, the hardness of training increased. They were whipped in public for misconduct, but whipping was also a technique of training leadership to develop courage and endurance. The cadets were also trained for secret services. They spied on the enemies and on the restless slaves as well.

After the cadet-training, there followed another period of service in an army garrison. It continued to the age of thirty. It was at this age that the soldier was admitted to full citizenship and was allowed to marry. The marriage, however, did not mean freedom for him to live with his wife all the time, for he continued to live in barracks and instructed boys. He was called to war if the need arose.

Education of Women

One progressive feature of the Spartan system of education was the gymnastic training, given to the girls and women. Since they were expected to become mothers of strong children, they needed to develop strong bodies. Although the girls were not herded into packs, they underwent the same training as the boys. They cultivated the moral strength and patriotism with which they supported their soldier husbands and sons at the time of war.

The process of education reflects the view that the Spartans had very little regard for literary and artistic studies. However, laws were memorised and selections from the Greek poet, Homer, were read. The youth also listened to stories of exploits and defeats, narrated by older people. Music was studied to develop hardness and not refinement. Thus, the Spartan system of education succeeded in producing the preferred type of citizens who were dare-devils. But the Spartan education made little contribution to art, literature, science, philosophy and government. The education was narrow in outlook and did not encourage novelty and progress. Rather it crushed individuality. The Spartans did not have legacies in areas of human endeavours other than, perhaps, the art of war.

The People in Attica (Athens)

There were about fifty thousand citizens in Attica in the middle of the fifth century B.C. At the age of eighteen, a boy provided that both his parents were Athenian citizens, took an oath and thereupon became a citizen with the right to attend the assembly.[4]

There were nearly twenty thousand Metics or foreigners who lived permanently in Athens. They were expected to fight in war and to pay a special tax, but they could not attend the assembly nor became magistrates. They were also not allowed to own property but they enjoyed freedom and shared in the commercial prosperity of Athens, which attracted so many of them to settle there.

There were slaves too, who were one hundred thousand in number. Although they were not citizens, they were an important feature of the Athenian way of life. Some of them were used to act as permanent secretaries to the magistrates and kept records. The entire police force consisted of slaves but they were dependent on the orders of the magistrate. Perhaps the Athenian citizen regarded police work of a lower kind, which for them was unattractive and unsuitable. Thus, the slaves were very important to the Athenian way of life. Besides some of the jobs mentioned here, they did many other kinds of work which were unpleasant to the Athenians. They worked in silver mines and as peasants, but were often paid by their masters.[5]

Education in Attica (Athens)

Education in Attica can be divided into two periods. Education during the earlier period was given through the ethenic practices. Education of the later period represented changes and innovations which made Athens the great fount of ideas. This was the period when great teachers and philosophers made contributions. In Attica education was a necessity for its citizens, but the State allowed the individuals a great deal of freedom. For example, the child at birth was examined by the father for fitness and not by other elders as in the case of Spartans. The father decided whether to preserve the child or to expose him to death.

The family brought up the boys and girls together up to the age of seven. Mothers and nurses cared for the children. After the age of seven, the girls stayed with their mothers, but the boys went to various teachers to acquire education.

Aim of Education

The aim of Athenian education was to provide boys courage and wisdom, but neither of these in excess. Boys were to be prepared both for war and peace. They were to be cultured citizens—broadly educated, refined, sensitive, civic-minded and moral beings. The aim was realised by sending boys to different teachers to acquire a wide variety of knowledge; expected of an Athenian youth.

The Process of Education

The boy went to a teacher called a 'grammatist'—someone like a primary school teacher in our modern times. Under him, the boy learnt reading, writing and counting. He learnt first the letters, then syllables and finally words. Reading was a difficult task as words and sentences were not as well organised as they are today. Great importance was paid to reading and literature. Recitation and acting were practised. Science and philosophy were also studied. There were no books so the teachers dictated their lessons and pupils wrote down or even memorised them. From the grammatist the boys moved to the music school. The teacher in the music school taught recitation of poetry and gave a special course in music when the boy had attained the age of thirteen. The instrument used was called a 'lyre'; it resembled a guitar. The flute was also used, but it was not popular. The music was to smooth, to purge and to harmonize man so that he became a moral person.[6]

Poetry and music went hand in hand to form a single art. The purpose was to prepare boys to develop well-balanced personalities and not to train them as professional musicians or poets. Professional playing was considered unworthy of a citizen and was left mainly to the foreigners and the slaves.

Another school that the boy attended was the 'palaestra' or gymnasium. Here boys between the ages of eight and sixteen played games and took part in sports. Again, the aim was not simply physical growth or victory in competitions but harmonious development by participating in the acts gracefully.

The ultimate end of all these activities was to exercise control of oneself. There were competitions, but the deciding factor was how well one played the game, no matter whether one won or lost. Simple exercise such as running was meant for younger children, while leaping, jumping, throwing the discus and casting the javelin, swimming and dancing were for the older boys. The exercises were done in classes and groups to the tune of music and were closely supervised by the teachers. This period of physical training ended at the age of sixteen and was controlled by the teachers and the family as well. For poor boys, this was a final education, but for boys from rich families, education continued until the age of twenty.

The idea behind this advanced stage in education was to train citizens to take up government offices. The training was in athletics in a state gymnasium. Two additional years were spent in military service when the youth took part in drills, camping in the open, learning army discipline and marching in public processions. He learnt the geography of the country and passed examinations to prove his worth. Then, he took an oath of loyalty to the State, gods and moral traditions.

As can be seen, the Athenian education was learning by doing rather than learning from books. The teacher, who was seldom paid by the State, played an important role in that. It was he who spoke, dictated, demonstrated, supervised and evaluated the learner. Most of the Athenian education was liberal and contributed to the all-round development of the citizen. It did not, however, consider women equal to men, either for training or for other citizenship duties.

The period of later Athenian education is marked with most memorable changes which took place after the Persian wars. In earlier years the education was mainly concerned with training men, but later on it became more concerned with training boys to become effective and successful. In order to achieve the new goals, the 'Sophists' made their way into Athens.[7]

The Sophists

In fact, the Sophists were a class of people (probably in the fourth century B.C.) who could impart quickly every kind of knowledge. The Sophists dealt whole-heartedly with the intellectual food. Sophists such as Euthydemus, Prodicus and Protagoras were known as 'the wisest of all living beings' and 'the only professors of moral improvement.'

Much has been written about the Sophists in the histories of philosophy and education, but hardly any group of teachers would have suffered more badly because of poor and bad publicity than the Sophists. 'Conventional opinion', says Edward J. Power, 'along with some respected testimony, often reveals the Sophists as ignorant, evil, pretentious, greedy men who came to Athens to beguile and exploit a gullible people and lead them along fraudulent path-ways to what they thought would be knowledge and political wisdom'.[8]

But despite much criticism and Plato's convincing condemnations, the Sophists must not be dismissed as frail figures in the history of education in Greece. As teachers they brought much educational progress. They were responsible for organising the first secondary schools with educational and intellectual purposes, and took the boys away from the gymnasium into the classrooms.

Truly speaking, the most characteristic development of Greek philosophy took form with the Sophists, who were known as the travelling teachers of wisdom. Will Durant remarks: 'They were all clever men (Gorgias and Hippias for example), and many of them were profound (Protagoras, Prodicus); there is hardly any problem or a solution in our current philosophy of mind and conduct which they did not realise and discuss.'[9]

Yet they lacked many things. Their teaching was unsystematic and was also limited to the few who could pay them for the tuition. The fact that they accepted payments for their teaching created dislike and prejudice against them. The few who could pay, obtained superiority over their fellow-citizens. All this led to violent outbursts and dislikes among those who could not educate themselves for lack of ability to pay.

Besides, they moved from place to place in search of students. They would advertise their product and exaggerate their abilities as teachers. As a result of this 'the masters of the permanent schools in Athens began to lose students to them. This, as a consequence, brought resentment against them from those masters.'

The prejudice against the Sophists was further intensified as they seemed to be degrading knowledge by making its aim direct utility. Plato seemed to have a special dislike for the Sophists who 'taught disputation without ethical consideration.' He was critical of them for he thought that they taught virtue first without providing a fundamental intellectual education in the beginning. The Sophists, who had been popular in the educational arena in Athens for more than a century, began to lose their fame and it was sometime then that Socrates started rising in the intellectual horizon of Athens.

Socrates (469-399 B.C.)

Socrates was born in or about 469 B.C. His father, Sophroniscus, was a friend of the family of Aristides the Just, who was the founder of the Delian League.

Socrates was married, apparently late in life, to Xenothippe, by whom he left three sons. His sons, according to Aristotle, proved insignificant.

He did not take part in politics because he did not want to compromise with his principles, but he is reported to have served as a hoplite, perhaps at Samos (440 B.C.) and at several other stations during the Peloponnesian war.

In 399 B.C. Socrates was indicted for 'impiety'. There were two charges against him. 'Corruption of the young and neglect of gods whom the city worshiped.' He was convicted, probably by 280 votes against 220. In the beginning they proposed a smaller penalty but since Socrates claimed that he was an eminent public benefactor too, it annoyed the court and death was voted by an increased majority. As a rule of Athens, a condemned man had to drink the poison, hem-lock. He did so, and became immortal.

Socrates as a Philosopher

Will Durant remarks: 'If we may judge from the bust that has come down to us as part of the ruins of ancient sculpture, Socrates was as far from being handsome as even a philosopher can be. A bald head, a great round face, deep-set staring eyes, a broad and flowery nose that gave vivid testimony to many a symposium—it was rather the head of a porter than that of the most famous of philosophers. But if we look again we see, through the crudity of the stone, something of that human kindness and unassuming simplicity which made this homely thinker a teacher beloved of the finest youths in Athens.'[10]

When Socrates was in his early twenties his thoughts turned away from the cosmological speculations towards man himself. There had been philosophers before him but for the most part they had been physical philosophers. They had sought for the nature of external things. Socrates said that it was good to think about the nature of external things but there was yet a worthier subject for philosophers than all that speculation about 'trees, stones and stars', and that was 'what is man, and what can he become?'

The Athenian youths liked best in him the modesty of his wisdom. 'He did not claim to have wisdom, but only to seek it lovingly; he was wisdom's amateur, not its' professional'.[11] Chaerephon, a devoted friend of his asked the 'Delphic Oracle' if there was any man living who was wiser than Socrates and received the answer 'No'. But Socrates was very modest and wise and he never forgot to show his ignorance on matters which were beyond his knowledge.

'There is no real philosophy until the mind turns round and

examines itself', Socrates thought. Philosophy begins when one learns to doubt one's cherished beliefs and one's dogmas. Socrates did not know that with such notions he was interpreting the agnostic dogmas long before agnosticism came into being.

K.R. Popper describes Socrates as the champion of the 'Open Society' of democracy; he was a man who emphasized the equalitarian theory of human reason as a universal medium for the communication of all ideas and principles; a philosopher who, in a time of utter sophistry and intellectual dishonesty, laid great stress on self-searching and self-criticism; a supporter of a strictly egalitarian theory of justice; a moralist who proposed that it is better to be the victim of injustice than to inflict injustice upon others; an individualist who propounded a creed of individualism and preached a belief in human individual as an end in himself.[12]

The Socratic Method

Gradually Socrates came to conceive of his mission as being to discover the stable and certain truth including true wisdom. He would enlist the aid of any man who would be ready to listen to him. He would go from man to man enquiring and questioning. If men discussed of justice, he asked them quickly—'what is it?' 'What do you mean by these abstract words with which you so easily settle the problems of life and death? What do you mean by honour, virtue, morality, patriotism? What do you mean by yourself ?'[13]

This method of enquiry, which we call the Socratic method, involved accurate definitions and clear thinking and left man's mind more confused than before. He would generally ask more than he answered. Ghester G. Starr reflecting on Socratic method writes:

> 'To begin this story one must go back to the great, if somewhat dim figure of Socrates who spent life in questioning the standards of his fellow Athenians. In doing so he developed the famous Socratic Method, which consisted of probing a man's beliefs and showing their inconsistency so as to reduce the victim to an admission of his own ignorance, the first step towards true wisdom.'

Robert R. Rusk remarks that the Socratic method or discourses consist of three stages. The first is called 'opinion', in which the individual is unable to give valid reasons for his assumed knowledge. The second is the destructive or the 'analytic stage', in which the individual is brought to realise that he does not knew what he thought he knew. It leads to contradiction, doubt or perplexity. The third is the 'synthetic stage', which Plato would call 'knowledge'. When this stage is reached the individual's experience is reconstructed and his beliefs justified.

According to Aristotle, Socrates contributed mainly in two ways—his inductive discourses and his universal definitions. Socrates thought that every term such as 'good', 'beautiful', 'justice' or 'man' has an unequivocal denotation. These terms or names, which are inaccessible to sense perception, are apprehensible only by thought. Such an object Socrates called an 'Idea' or 'Eidos' or a 'Form'.

The universal definition is an attempt to formulate the meaning of a universally significant predicate i.e. a 'form'.

The 'inductive arguments' means the way to arrive at such formulations (Forms) by way of simple but concrete illustrations. All this made Socrates unforgetable and created for him a position which has been reached so far by very few in the realm of philosophy.

Socratic Ethics and Religion

Like the Sophists Socrates also condemned the ancient polytheistic faith. He felt that to follow those beliefs would be a 'hopeless and suicidal policy'. It would be a progress backwards. Socrates had his own religious beliefs. He believed in one God and disowned all the gods and goddesses of Olympus.

He had a desire to build a system of morality which would be independent by helping men to reach a stage where he would have a clear sight with which they could reach peace, order and good will.

Socrates felt, '... if men could be taught to see clearly their real interests, to see as far as the distant results of their deeds, to criticise and coordinate their desires out of a self-cancelling chaos into a purpose and creative harmony—this perhaps, would provide for the morality which in the unlettered relies on reiterated precepts and external control. Perhaps all sin is error, partial vision foolishness?'[14]

Socrates disapproved of superstitious beliefs and wanted men to seek wisdom with unhindered thought. Men could reach the realms of morality, justice and goodness by uncovering their own assumptions and questioning their certainties.

Socrates' Influence on Education

It is from Plato that we obtained almost everything about Socratic thought for Plato was one of his closest admirers.

Although it would not be too easy to accept all Platonic conclusions about Socrates, the presumption remains that ethical theorizing was accelerated greatly by the activities of Socrates. Besides his ethical theories, he also cannot be forgotten for his ethical content, and both his ethical theories and content have relevance to educational theory.

Another great contribution of Socrates is his method, which we call 'Socratizing'. For centuries, that followed Socrates, it has been accepted and praised as a teacher's most effective technique.

Truly speaking, Socratic method is a scientific one which has greatly influenced the educationists and scientists alike. His inductive arguments have enlightened men in all centuries and countries.

Plato (427-347 B.C.)

Plato belonged to an old and distinguished family which had a good number of political connections in Athens. Little is known of his early life but it is assumed by the historians that he received his normal education of a Greek youth; that of learning to read and write and pursuing a study of the poets.[15]

Plato grew up in Athens. It was the time of the Peloponnesian War, which lasted from 431 to 403 B.C. and resulted in defeat and humiliation for Athens. This was followed by a reign of terror and tyranny for eight months until the democratic constitution was once more restored. It was this democracy that put Socrates to death in the year 399 B.C. on the charges of impiety and corrupting the young. This event had a deep and lasting effect upon Plato, who had expected to go into politics, but he became disgusted with it all and drew back, as he says, from the wickedness of the times.[16]

Plato's own disillusionment at the political scene led him to think that all existing States were poorly governed and they needed to be really reformed. Probably, when Plato was quite young he met Socrates who left a great deal of influence on him. Therefore, he thought that the only hope of finding justice for either an individual or society at large could be found in true philosophy, and "until philosophers are kings, or the kings and princess of this world have the spirit and power of philosophy, and political greatness and wisdom meet in one, and those commoner natures who pursue either to the exclusion of the other are compelled to stand aside, cities will never have rest from their evils—no, nor the human race, as I believe—and then only will this our State have a possibility of life and behold the light of day."[17]

Plato travelled in several different countries including Cyrene and Egypt. He also served in the Athenian Army. It was between 388 - 387 B.C. that he visited Southern Italy and came in touch with Pythagorean philosophers, who orientated him in the Orphie-Pythagorean belief that there is an 'after-life' and mathematics is a philosophic discipline.[18]

A year after his visit to Italy, he founded the famous Academy where he taught until his death in 347 B.C. The main object of his Academy or the 'University' was to train politicians, who would become the sort of philosopher ruler described in 'the 'Republic'.

It was here in the Academy that Plato sought to continue the work of Socrates and taught philosophy. He went on seeking his perfect philosopher-king of his dreams in his Academy on the lines stated in the Republic until he died.

Plato's Philosophy

Plato thought that the ills of society could not be eliminated until philosophers ruled the State. Therefore, the education of such philosophers became most important for him. The *Republic* is a statement of that aim i.e. to train philosophers—statesmen. The Ideal State, described in the *Republic,* is to be governed by philosophers, so philosophy itself plays a large part in the *Republic.* The philosophy contained in the *Republic* expresses Plato's belief in Two Worlds. 'There is the every-day, physical world in which we live; there is the world of eternals, of absolutes, 'ideas' or 'Forms'. It is important that the philosopher should have a true sense of values: these values are absolute, and their ultimate source and standard is 'Absolute Goodness, or the Form of the Good'.[19]

Plato reflects that the vision of the Form of the Good is something what some people have described as 'the vision of God'. But it does not mean that the Form of the Good and God are necessarily the same. The experience of the Form of the Good is mystical or even religious. It is a sort of 'a state of knowledge' but difficult of being communicated in ordinary language.

According to Plato the Form of the Good is supreme and is the source of the existence of all other Forms. He compared the Good to the sun which is the source of light and growth and gives visibility to the objects of sense. Like the sun, the Good is the source of Truth and Reality and it provides intelligibility to the objects of thought and power to the faculty of knowledge, which is the mind.

Plato thinks that the physical world is a World of Opinion, in which both Illusion and Belief play their part. Illusion consists of images and shadows, but as one goes higher up one gets into the realm of Belief, which is concerned with the sense-objects, or physical things. The Intelligible World is the realm of knowledge, which at the lower levels uses the objects of the physical world as illustrations, but the highest knowledge is to be found in the 'dialectic', which according to Plato is the pure thought which transcends the physical world and recognises the realm of Form and 'ideas'.

The Simile of the Cave in the *Republic* in Book VII, provides a more vivid picture of the Platonic metaphysics.[20]

'Behold! human beings living in an underground den which has a mouth open towards the light and reaching all along the den; they have been here from their childhood, and have their legs and necks chained so that they cannot move, and can only see before them; for the chains are arranged in such a manner as to prevent them turning round their heads. Above and behind them the light of a fire is blazing at a distance, and between the fire and the prisoners there is a raised way.'

There is a low wall built along the way, just like a screen over which players might show their puppets. There are moving figures, who hold various objects made of wood and stone. The prisoners can see only their own shadows or the shadows of one another created on the wall by the fire. Likewise, they see the shadows of the objects which are being carried by the moving figures.

Thus, the metaphor describes the conditions under which we lead our lives like prisoners—the only knowledge we can have of the events outside us is that of the shadows cast by these events. The sounds we hear are vague and confused. This is the illusory perception of the world from which only a few can ascend to Pure Thought or the highest realm of knowledge. Only a true philosopher can have such a true vision.

True knowledge, according to Plato is eternal and unchanging. He does not reject the physical phenomena of sense-experience but describes it as having no reality. Physical objects or phenomena derive their reality from the Form of which they are merely copies. Thus, Plato's doctrine of Form or Ideas has traditionally been known as 'Idealism', some try to seek 'realism' in his philosophy as they think that his ideas are 'real' because they have an absolute existence outside the mind of man. The fact is that Plato in his outlook and philosophical reflections, such as the Simile of the Cave, seeks the Idealistic doctrine which is further confirmed by his concepts of Forms.

Plato on Education

It is in Plato's *Republic* that his chief treatment of education can be discovered. Rousseau reflected: If you wish to know what is meant by public education, read Plato's *Republic.* Those who merely judge books by their titles take this for a treatise on Politics, but it is the finest treatise on education ever written.[21]

"Plato's principal educational objectives", says Power, "did not differ from those accepted in early Athens or, for that matter, from those considered orthodox in Sparta. He aimed at good citizenship".[22] He thought that competence in civic affairs was of prime importance. One could possess citizenship if one knew the proper system of values and had profound knowledge and understanding which could lead to wisdom. All this could be achieved only through education.

Plato believed strongly in the principle of Recollection. 'The vision of Truth and Goodness were, in fact, already within us; it was largely a question of the teacher helping to turn the eye of his students inward towards the light![23] Thus, according to Plato the true art of teaching lies in setting the light objectives before the pupil so that his vision may be cleared and understanding sharpened. He is to be led to the 'Vision of Goodness' which is already within him.

Keeping these objectives in mind, Plato applies the principle of the division of labour. He separates the citizens of his Ideal State into two classes—the industrial or artisan, and the guardian class. The duty of the artisan class is to provide the necessaries of life and the duty of the guardians is to enlarge the boundaries of the state. The guardian class is further subdivided into the military and governing classes, representing the respective rules in the government service.

In the *Republic,* Plato provided an appropriate form of training to the soldier and the ruler or philosopher classes of people, but no mention is made of the education of the industrial class. There could be no specific training in citizenship, for these members of the community have no voice in the government of the state; their characteristic virtue is obedience, technically temperance—to know their place and to keep it.[24] Perhaps, it was his aristocratic prejudice which could have been instrumented by the Greek contempt for the mechanical arts that his educational scheme in the *Republic* is confined to guardian class only. It was much later when he had grown older that in the *Laws,* he considers that education is to be universal, not restricted to the guardian class and is to be compulsory, whether the parents please or they do not, 'the children shall come to the school.'

Both in the *Republic* and the *Laws*, Plato reflects that the pupils shall be regarded as belonging to the state rather than to the parents. This law applies to females as well as males. This communistic ideal, which he projected in the *Republic* that children are the property of the state, is re-emphasised in the *Laws*. In the *Republic* as well as in the *Laws* the state is made responsible for the education of the children. Plato, therefore, is blamed for forerunning the communistic ideal long before the spread of communism.

The Curriculum

The main subjects proposed in the curriculum in the *Laws* and in the *Republic*, are the same. 'For early education music and gymnastics and for the higher education mathematics, dialectic, the study to which the mathematical subjects were merely preparatory in the *Republic*, is alluded to only indirectly in the more practical Laws'.[25]

Scheme of Early Education

At the outset of his treatment of education he asserts that education of children should start with music first and proceed thereafter to gymnastics. He wants mental to proceed physical education. Reflecting about the education of the young children, Plato requires that the authorised tales only are to be narrated to them by their mothers and nurses and the tales which the young children first hear should be models of virtuous thoughts. Thus, Plato reaffirms at each stage of the training that nothing must be admitted in education which does not promote virtue. The fables, consisting of themes of gods and heroes, convey truth; temperance, obedience and self-control only.

Plato maintained that while teaching music such harmonies, which make the citizens temperate and courageous, should be retained. He thought that musical training was 'a more potent instrument than any other, because rhythm and harmony find their way into the inward places of the soul' and bring grace to the educated.

Plato's discussion on gymnastics in the *Republic* is very brief. He prescribed a moderate system which could bring forth good health. He does not approve of much indulgence in physical exercises for he reflects that one who involves too much in gymnastics 'is like a wild beast, all violence and fierceness and knows no other way of dealing; and he lives in all ignorance...'.

However, gymnastics occupies a more important place in the *Laws* than it does in the *Republic*. He divides it into two branches, dancing and wrestling, which bring agility and beauty in the limbs, and energy and strength respectively.

Without prescribing any training in the manual arts, which he reckoned mean, Plato concludes the scheme of early education, limiting it to the training in music and gymnastics only.

Scheme of Higher Education

Plato does not entitle all to get higher education. Only 'the surest and the bravest, and if possible, the fairest' are to be provided with higher education. The aim of higher education is not merely extension of knowledge but a wider understanding of the real world. The higher education includes number or arithmetic, plane and solid geometry, astronomy, theory of music or harmonies. These are the subjects which lead one to reach the highest ladder of education, namely, dialectic.

The principles, which made Plato decide to select the subjects of higher education, were that they must lead to reflection rather than deal with things of sense and be of universal application. Thus, the main function of number, more than the practical needs, is to afford a training in abstraction. Plato thinks that training in one function (number) results in a general improvement of the mind. This would help improving other functions. In this way he was implying the doctrine of formal discipline.

Plato believes that the study of geometry would bring quick apprehension and draw the soul towards truth. After geometry, he suggests the study of astronomy which could be of great use to the agriculturist and navigators, and above all, could lead to improve the reasoning faculty. Next to astronomy is music, which at this stage of education involves the theory of music, including harmonies and the mathematical relations, existing between notes, chords, etc.

Study of Dialectic

Philosophy or Dialectic is the highest study for Plato. It proceeds without presuppositions and seeks critically to examine the validity and truth about things. It has the power to reveal the absolute truth.

Plato, in the *Republic,* reflects that dialectic is the coping stone of the sciences; it is an eye to the soul, which brings a clear understanding of the actual truth. Therefore, it is considered the highest study in his scheme of education of the rulers.

Distribution of Studies

After considering the subjects for the philosopher-kings, Plato decides the distribution of studies.

Early education should be completed at the age of sixteen. For three years, after the early education, that is, from seventeen to twenty years of age, he wants the youths to serve as cadets, to be brought to the battle-field and to do plenty of bodily service but indulging in no intellectual study.

At the age of twenty the chosen students are to undergo the study of mathematics and other subjects prescribed for higher education. This training should continue for ten years after which the selected ones begin the study of *dialectic* which should continue for five years. For the next fifteen years soldiers or rulers should return to practical life and take the command in war and hold offices of state which could befit them. This takes them to the age of fifty when they spend their lives in the pursuit of truth or 'The Good'.

Such is the scheme of education proposed by Plato in the *Republic* and the *Laws* as well. As for women, he proposed the same education which he designed for men, for he felt that women in general are equal to men in almost all spheres. Therefore, befitting education and jobs should be provided to them.

Plato's Influence

Plato's influence on later educational thought and practice can be seen at different times. Quintilian, in his curriculum, considered music, arithmetic, geometry and astronomy important for study at school.

According to Whitehead, Platonic views have encouraged the study of art and brought in the importance and dignity of mind against the matter.

Plato's Academy was really the first University in Europe. His 'schemes of education' were so appealing that not only in the medieval period but the post-medieval times as well they were accepted, though with slight changes.

There is no doubt that Plato is blamed for creating for his Ideal State a society of classes and a 'totalitarian scheme', which could have influenced the communists or the Nazis and would lead to the ideal of 'indoctrination', but he presented a formal scheme of education which is being practised even today.

Above all, Plato in his *Republic,* except the study of technical education, presented that education should aim at the ideal of 'citizenship' and 'leadership'. It should lead to intellectual growth and enlighten pupils to find the actual truth or 'The Good'; it should lead to perfect self-development and help reaching the stage of self-realization, which is the ideal of Idealistic philosophy.

Plato is also known as the forerunner of the idea of equal opportunities for both sexes and to bring into the realm of education the growth of moral, religious and social aspects, which could fit into the schemes of education of all the developing countries of the world at all times.

Aristotle (384-322 B.C.)

Aristotle was born at Stagira, a city in Macedon, about two hundred miles away from Athens, in the year 384 B.C. His father was a friend and physician to the king of Macedon. There are many stories of his youth. According to one narrative, in his early life he indulged in riotous living, joining the army to avoid starvation. Later on he returned to Stagira to practise medicine and went to Athens at the age of thirty to study philosophy under Plato.[26]

Some accounts convey that he studied under the great master for twenty years. But the pervasive Platonism of Aristotle's speculations suggests that he remained Plato's disciple for a much longer period.[27] Therefore, Plato had a tremendous influence on his as an incomparable teacher, who indoctrinated him in the realms of philosophy and morality, making him excel on the horizon of philosophy and education for many centuries to come.

After his completion of education with the great master, Aristotle's fame won him the tutorship of Alexander, whom he taught philosophy and politics. But, when Alexander, who had gone to conquer Asia, died there, Aristotle was left out without a patron. He, then, returned to Athens in the year 334 B.C., but was denounced there to be associated with the Macedonian group. He fled away from there, arrived at Chalcis, and fell ill. In utter disappointment, he committed suicide by drinking hem-lock.

Aristotle's Metaphysics

Aristotle thinks that all the things of the world are moved by an inner urge to become something greater. Form has grown out of matter, out of which still higher forms have grown. He thinks, 'man is the form of which the child was the matter; the child is the form, and its embryo the matter; they reach the thought of matter which has no form. Such a formless matter would be nothing, for everything must have a form. Therefore, matter is the possibility of form, which is the reality. Form is the inner impulse which moulds and shapes the matter into a specific figure.

Aristotle thinks that everything in the world moves naturally due to a specific course or fulfilment. Development is not accidental but guided in a certain direction from within by its nature. The egg of a hen is internally designed to become a chick and not a duck. But this does not make Aristotle think that there is an external force or providence which is shaping earthly structures or making events happen. The design is always internal.[28]

But with this sort of reflection Aristotle does not think that there is no God. There is a God, who created motion. He is the source of motion. He is a 'prime mover' but He is unmoved. Aristotle conceived God as a being who is in-visible, spaceless, sexless, passionless, changeless, perfect and eternal.[29] Aristolian God does not create anything but moves the world as the total motive of all operations in the world. He is the final cause of nature. He is the drive of all things and is the form of the world. He is the sum of its vital powers and the eternal and inherent goal of its growth.

Thus, Aristotle's God is a mysterious spirit for He never does anything. He does not have any desire or will. Though He is absolutely perfect, but He cannot desire anything, therefore, He does nothing and creates nothing. Aristotle loved philosophy and contemplated so much that he did not think that he was sacrificing his conception of divinity. His God is quite his type who is withdrawn to an ivory tower and is away from the strife and turmoil of the world.

His Views on Education

Aristotle conducted one of Athens famous schools called *Lyceum*. After he had broken ties with Plato's Academy, Lyceum occupied his most of the time. It was there in that school that 'he laid the foundations for, and advanced progress in, a number of academic and scientific fields'.[30]

He reflected that 'all art and education aim at filling up nature's deficiencies'.[31] Aristotle recognised that an individual has intellectual, moral and physical qualities and all these qualities or capacities are to be developed in him. An educational programme, based on the principles of developing the above capacities, could be considered worthwhile.

He also mentioned that good habits must be formed through care and exercise. Since he acclaimed that the general function of education is to direct men towards happiness, care must be taken to develop the intellectual and moral qualities. He added that education of men must be state-controlled so that they are provided the right kind of experience. In this way he authorised the state to mould the youths according to the objectives of the state so that it could utilise them for its benefit and growth. Aristotle totally rejected the idea of private-tutoring.

Aristotle had quite different views from his master about the education of women. He thought: 'woman is to man as the slave to the master, the manual to the mental worker, the barbarian to the Greek. Woman is an unfinished man, left standing on a lower step in the scale of development'.[32] He thought that the male is superior by nature and the female is inferior, therefore, she is incapable of independence of position. Her best position is a peaceful home-life in which she may be supreme.

Like his master, he accepted music and gymnastics as the subjects to be taught at the primary level. The former helps framing good moral habits and the later builds good bodies. But more than the choice of subjects and organisation of schools at primary, secondary and higher levels, he was interested in the theory of education and the philosophic principles. He was vitally concerned about the kinds of virtues which need to be formed in the school environment. But he suggested very little how those virtues could be achieved.

Aristotle's Influence

Aristotle did not reach the height in thought and fame as his master Plato achieved. We find him less enthusiastic about everything. He did not have either the reforming zeal nor love for humanity, which Plato had. Neither had he the originality which was possessed by his master. But still his creation of a new discipline of thought, that is 'logic', and his firm establishment of its essential lines, wins him lasting fame.

Although he did not put much stress on experimental and fruitful hypothesis in the domain of natural science, he is well known for the collection and classification of data. He influenced 'the ways of quest' in modern sciences, specially biological sciences.

Although Aristotle's ethics is a branch of his logic, he provides us a list of propriety useful to attain the moral realm.

Aristotle had his own prejudice against educating women and perhaps Rousseau owned some of his views from him, but he did not hesitate to recognise women supreme in domestic affairs.

He did not pay much attention to the organisational aspects of schools and was less concerned with the number of subjects to be taught at various levels, but he produced a theory of education which has come down to us from his times. None before him had recognised that 'all art and education aim at filling up nature's deficiencies'. This sort of belief has been accepted as an important theory in education by all the progressive countries of the world.

REFERENCES

1. Chaster G. Starr (1968), *The Awakening of the Historical Spirit* (New York: Alfred A. Knopf, Inc.), pp. 1-42.
2. Bowen James (1972), *A History of Western Education* (London: Methuen & Co.), p. 51-52.
3. J.A. Bury (1922), *A History of Greece* (New York: St. Martin's Press, Inc.), p. 135.
4. Robin Barrow (1973), *Athenian Democracy* (London: Macmillan Edu. Ltd.), p. 42-46.
5. Robin, *Athenian Democracy*, p. 42-46.
6. Power Edward J. (1970), *Main Currents in the History of Education* (New York: McGrew Hill Co.), p. 50-53.
7. Power, *History of Education*, p.73.
8. Power, *History of Education*, p. 76.
9. Durant Will (1970), *The Story of Philosophy*, (New York: Washington Sq. Press), p. 3.
10. Durant, *Story of Philosophy*, pp. 4-5.
11. Durant, *Story of Philosophy*, p. 6.
12. Popper, K.R. (1966), *The Open Society and its Enemies*, p. 119, Vol. 1. *The Spells of Plato* 5th Ed. (London: Routledge) pp. 189-94.
13. Durant, *Story of Philosophy*, p. 6.
14. Durant, *Story of Philosophy*, p. 8.
15. Boyd, W. (1964), *The History of Western Education*, (London: A&C Black) pp. 1-42.
16. Morrish Ivor, (1976), *Discipline of Education*, (London: George Allen & Unwin Ltd.) p. 55.
17. Jowett, B. (tr.) (1928), *The Republic of Plato*, Third Edition, O.U.P.
18. Morrish, *Discipline of Education*, pp. 57-58.
19. Morrish, *Discipline of Education*, p. 59.
20. Plato (1964), *The Republic*, (Penguin Books; Pelican), Vol. VII, p. 514.
21. Rousseau, J.J. (1966), *EMILE* (Everyman edition), p. 8 (Tr. J.M. Dent).
22. Power, *History of Education*, p. 93.
23. Morrish, *Discipline of Education*, p. 68.
24. Lewis Campbell (1902), *Plato's Republic*, (London: John Murray), p. 54.
25. Rusk Robert R. (1969), *Doctrines of the Great Educators*, Fourth Edition (London: Macmillan), p. 31-32.
26. Durant, *Story of Philosophy*, p. 49.
27. Durant, *Story of Philosophy*, p. 49.
28. Durant, *Story of Philosophy*, p. 70.
29. Durant, *Story of Philosophy*, p. 71.
30. Power, *History of Education*, p. 113.
31. Aristotle, *Politics* vii, p. 17.
32. Aristotle, *Politics* iii, 3, vii 8.

CHAPTER-II

LIFE AND EDUCATION IN ROME

Education in Rome from 800 to 250 B.C.

Early Romans were a rural people. Even the aristocratic class of people devoted themselves to cultivation. Since most of the people were farmers, they did not expect much from education. If they thought to get anything from education it was to attain some cultural objectives. Thus, early Roman life was far from complicated. Because schools were not essential there were only a few schools. The family was considered to be the chief schooling agency, where education was realised in daily life.

Education, what so ever it was then, was boy-centred and the father was responsible for providing his son with the early education which was mainly the preparation for Roman life.

Education, which started from the family, went beyond it and every Roman had the ultimate goal of attaining many virtues—one of which was absolute devotion to the State.

It was up to the age of sixteen that a father was the principal teacher of his son but beyond that age several important changes took place in his training. One of the important changes was that in place of father an old friend or a relative, also a renowned person, was called in to educate the young man. As a young man he accompanied the new tutor place to place and learned much about the public life. Because the Roman youth became a citizen at sixteen, he did not need to wait to complete the military training for its attainment.

After attaining the citizenship, the next step in the preparation of the public man was the military service. A Roman, who had distinguished in military service, especially in war, got more respect and power in the State.

One of the important aspects of early Roman education was that both boys and girls were interested in physical fitness and sports.[1] Roman children took part in ball games, wrestling, running, hunting, jumping and cycling. Some of these sports were reckoned very useful for the ensuring military service. Besides, every Roman boy and girl knew swimming and dancing and enjoyed music but they did not have any gymnastics.

Education in Rome from 250 B.C. to 250 A.D.

It was the time when Roman empire was at its pinnacle as it annexed big territories of the neighbouring countries. 'With each new acquisition of territory, Rome met with cultural forces that affected her deeply.[2]

During this period Roman education underwent great changes which were mostly inspired by Greek models. Greek slaves, who were brought to Rome, were mostly made into teachers. So the Romans wanted teachers from Greece; they were willing to take any number of Greeks who could teach and encourage them to immigrate, to enter the teaching profession in Rome.[3]

Elementary Education

Although most of Roman education of their period was affected by Greek educational thought, the Romans tried to seek into their own past. There existed Roman schools besides the schools inspired by the Greeks. In these Roman schools Latin was taught and traditional Roman values were fostered. The schools with Greek influence, continued teaching of classical Greek. Thus, a duel system of schools came into existence.

It was not before the third century A.D. that the elementary school system became popular. Such schools were known as *ludus*, which meant sport, play or game.[4] A teacher in such schools was known as *litterator*, who taught reading, writing and calculation too. Elementary education started when boys and girls were about seven years and continued until they reached twelve. There were no good buildings available for the sports, so the teachers used either a porch or a booth for imparting education.

Secondary Education

In order to acquire good social position, boys and girls, after completing their elementary education, entered secondary schools where the *grammaticus* took their charge. There were special classrooms available for secondary schools. The *grammaticus* or the secondary school teacher wore a cloak which gave him prestige and importance. He knew grammar and literature well. Since secondary school system came into existence in

Rome only after the Greek influence, such schools consisted largely of the study of the Greek classics. Although works of Homer and Dionysius were translated into Latin and were read by Romans, Greek grammar and literature were very popular and mainly constituted the secondary school curriculum.

Higher Education System

Roman higher education was also mainly Greek education, having almost the higher schools based on the Hellenistic system and age.

After completing his studies in grammar in a secondary school, a Roman boy could go on to a higher school for the study of rhetoric which was aimed at to master the art of oratory. Rules of rhetoric, consisting of methods, were to be studied first and then practice in speaking began. Such 'schools of rhetoric' were presided by well known Latin teachers called the *rhetors*. A *rhetor* would wear precious garments and ran his school in a fine building. There were a few rhetors who were honoured with appointments in governments and some were paid their salaries by the State. Thus, such schools of rhetoric were mostly independent institutions of a special kind where higher studies were pursued.

A Roman boy started rhetorical study at the age of fifteen and completed it when he was about twenty. At this stage formal education of the Romans ended.

It was after this education that they were ready to enter public life and to serve the State in various positions. But if any Roman boy wanted to study further he could continue the study of oratory or could take up law, medicine or philosophy.

Roman boys liked to continue the study of law rather than rhetoric. In fact, Roman law was the great creation of the Roman genius[5], and as time passed, the study of law became more complex, difficult and prestigious. The teachers, who taught law were often held in high honour. They were elected sometimes after an examination or after giving specimen lessons, by the local committees, with religious ceremonies and took an oath of office on entering upon their duties.[6]

Although education was State-controlled, it was never made compulsory and the State did not support it. Education was mainly supported by some important wealthy persons. When Rome became a Republic, it encouraged education more. Under Augustus education was given even further encouragement, and when a decree was proclaimed for the banishment of all foreigners from Rome, teachers and physicians were allowed to stay.[7] This was the time when Cicero and Quintilian came over the Roman horizon with their pedagogical theories and rhetoric rules which were hitherto unknown to the Romans.

Mareus Tullius Cicero (106-43 B.C.)

Mareus Tullius Cicero influenced the Roman education during the latter part of the Republic. He was a leading orator and statesman of Rome and expert both in rhetoric and philosophy. He not only wrote on rhetoric and philosophy but on politics and education as well.

Although Cicero was not an educator, his educational views contained in *De Oratore* expressed the ideas of an educated man about the purpose and methods of education. As a son of a Roman knight he had the privilege of receiving good education in Greek rhetoric and law. After serving in the army for some time, he became a pleader in the courts at the age of twenty-five. A few years later he became the greatest of Roman orators and a renowned writer of Roman literature.

Among Cicero's many other books such as *De Inventione*, *De Officiis* and *Brutus*, *De Oratore* is considered to be the most complete one which contains the fundamentals of his doctrine. It was published in 55 B.C. and contained all that Cicero felt necessary for an orator's education.

In *De Oratore*, Cicero maintained that an orator needed a broad, well-sounded and general education in the liberal arts, which could make the orator proficient in the art of oratory. He included, under the study of the liberal arts, the study of grammar, literature, logic, astronomy, music, physics, geometry, law, history and philosophy. He was the first Roman educator who prescribed the study of history as a valuable study, more especially the national history.

De Oratore, being an essay on oratory, mainly contained his teaching of rhetoric.

Marcus Fabius Quintilian (A.D. 35-97)

Marcus Fabius Quintilian was born in Spain about A.D. 35. He received education in Rome and returned to Spain when he was twenty five years old. After almost two years of his coming back to Spain, he was invited to return to Rome. In Rome, he acted as a pleader in the courts. He also taught rhetoric and obtained unusual success. In a few years he became a public teacher and was paid by the public treasury.

When Quintilian reached fifty three he retired from teaching and devoted himself to writing. His famous book, *Institutio Oratoria*, which contains 'how to educate an orator', was published in A.D. 96. This brought him abundant fame and honour. His theories on education, which knew no parallel for centuries, set a new pattern for Latin grammar schools appealing to the educators who followed him.

The book, *Institutio Oratoria* consists of twelve sections. Most parts of the book consist of discussion on rhetoric and the role it should play in secondary and higher education. Most of the parts of the book reflect one goal only, that is, educating young men for oratory. Quintilian's *Institutio Oratoria* soon came to be known as the final and standard book on the theory and practice of Roman Oratory, and that it is universally recognised as the most elaborate and complete treatise on Roman education ever written.[8]

Quintilian's Theory of Education

His Institutio Oratoria or *Education of an Orator* is more than a guide to the education of children. It contains a varied kind of discussion concerning teaching and learning from the child's early life until he becomes an accomplished orator.[9]

Quintilian is more concerned with the education of boys than girls. The whole of *Education of an Orator* is devoted to boys and not to girls.

He thinks that parents are greatly responsible for shaping a child's character. At the same time he recognises the importance of nurses who would play a great role in children's education. The parents' role is limited mainly to superintending the educational process while that of a nurse or a governess is extended to teaching during the most critical period of formation. Considering the importance of parents and nurses in respect of children, he expects both the parents and nurses to possess sound education.

Neither parents nor nurses are always supposed to be with their children. The children must be allowed time for free playing. Thus, children have free hours for leisure and recreation. But these free hours must not be left unguided or unguarded and even the companions of the child must be assessed and approved by the nurses.

Considering the importance of the early home training given by parents and nurses, he wants training to be fully formal as it is two-sided. One side is moral and the other is intellectual. Thus, his educational aim, that is, 'the excellence of character', is kept in view from the very beginning. Quintilian says, 'Young men should have their habits in the right living; and these habits come more from practice than from learning'.[10]

Quintilian believed that good impressions fade away earlier than the bad ones, so he would not allow any boy to become used to, even in his earliest years, to an incorrect style or manner of speech, which in later years could be forgotten easily. Therefore, he always expected the nurses and parents to be as highly educated as possible. He was quite aware of the role played by mothers in the early moral education of their children.

Throughout the twelve books (Institutio Oratoria) the methods of teaching recommended, lead the children to develop a general competence in oratory and eloquence. After being guided and trained properly in the manners of speech by the parents and nurses, the child at the age of seven goes to a school for further training. Qunitilian accepts age seven as the time for beginning schooling. He thinks that public schools are always better for instructions than the guidance of a private master.

Quintilian's theory of learning is comprised of two dimensions—formation and information. He believes that good methodology, which could help in the growth of intellectual abilities, will always retain the children's interest in learning.

He also believed that training and education could modify the weakness of nature and help improving faculties of memory, imagination and sense perception. Therefore, good care must be taken by teachers, and learning should proceed step by step. He asked teachers to use the techniques of drill, repetition and stimulation. He thought that drill was a way of reinforcing knowledge, so it must be used at the early stages of training.

While he approved of play and relaxation as important aspects of learning, he condemned corporal punishment. He rejected physical punishment for two reasons—it was fit for slaves and that it would bring repression in pupils and harden their attitude towards learning. Therefore, he directed that only good teachers, who could understand the psychology of their pupils, should be employed. The teachers must use competition and commendation as their tools of instructions and must not adhere to any kind of reproof or flogging.

Quintilian's Curriculum

Quintilian prescribed two kinds of schools—the grammar school, which needed to be attended after seven years of a child's age, and the school of rhetoric, which was to be attended after completion of the grammar school.

Children should reach the grammar school after they learnt reading and writing at the primary stage. Grammar schools should be assigned two tasks which were discharged by the grammarian: teaching the art of speaking correctly, and bringing home to the students the interpretations of the poets. With these two tasks, the theory of writing and the art of reading must be added.

Reading was always the most dependable way of getting knowledge of the carefully selected information. He also included the study of music, geometry and philosophy in the grammar school.

Besides the disciplinary value of music as it moulds the soul, Quintilian thought that instrumental and vocal music were useful to the future of an orator. Both could help refining his mode of expression, adding to grace and harmony in speech and movement. Thus, he justifies the teaching of music in grammar schools. Geometry too was accepted by him at this stage because it would develop logical skills and advance the knowledge of numbers and symbols.

Reflecting on the curriculum plan dealing with higher education, Quintilian prescribed the study of rhetoric. Teachers of rhetoric must begin their teaching where teachers of grammar stop, and care must be exercised to keep the boundaries between grammar and rhetoric clear and precise.[11]

The study of rhetoric contained the theory of eloquence and its practice. In addition to learning the theory of rhetoric, Quintilian reflected on those orators, poets and historians that students should read. The best ones were those who were clear in their style of writing and lucid in expression. One of these writers, according to Quintilian, was Cicero, whom he honoured as Rome's greatest orator and educator.

Quintilian's Influence

Quintilian exercised great influence in the educational arena for many centuries after his death. He believed that the great objective of instruction was to create mental activity. While teaching, the teachers must know the abilities of the pupils and plan the lessons accordingly. The main function of education was to correct the weakness in nature of the pupil, so the first year of his life needed careful supervision. He claimed that parents and nurses should be well educated and help in developing children's character.

It was Quintilian, who many centuries before John Locke and John Dewey, reflected the importance of variety of subjects and study. It was not Froebel but Quintilian who first claimed that play, recreation and relaxation were important at the early stages of child's growth.

Quintilian was far more than a genius who during the first century A.D. prescribed the study of the child's nature by careful observation. He reflected that the periods of play and rest were essential. He drew a list of qualities essential to become a good teacher. All such reflections can be considered useful at any time in the world.

REFERENCES

1. W.W. Fowler (1925), *The Roman Festivals of the Period of the Republic;* (New York: MacMillan), p. 35-40.
2. Power, *History of Education,* p. 154.
3. Gwynn Aubrey (1926), *Roman Education from Cicero to Quintilian* (New York: Oxford University Press), pp. 34-41.
4. Power, *History of Education,* p. 157.
5. W. Hghus Johns (1935), *A Brief History of Ancient Times;* (London: Ginn and Co.), p. 336-337.
6. Stabart, J.C. (1971), *The Grandeur that was Rome* (London: Sidgwick & Jackson), p. 259.
7. Power, *History of Education,* p. 166.
8. R.R. Bolgar, (1954), *The Classical Herita and its Beneficiaries;* (London: Cambridge University Press), p. 346.
9. Quintilian, *Institutio Oratoria,* Preface, p. 4-9.
10. Power, *History of Education,* p. 182.
11. Quintilian, *Oratoria II,* e.i. pp. 4-8.

CHAPTER-III

THE DAWN OF CHRISTIAN EDUCATION

For more than four centuries a school containing doctrines of the Christian faith and culture was unknown to Rome. Christian boys and girls attended either the secular schools or special Christian schools. The Christian schools prepared the prospective Christians merely for entrance into the church and ignored literary or linguistic objectives.

The Christian Church was indifferent to the ordinary literary education and refused to establish her own schools believing that literary culture was not important for the Christians. The mission of the church was documented by divine authority and, therefore, in comparison to the Christian goals which mainly included salvation, literary education was considered unfruitful.

At that time the first and the best instrument for advancing Christian education, was supposed to be the family, which was also considered a natural place for moral and religious teaching. This was the beginning of Christian education. The Christian family was the centre of the Christian educational beliefs and was a potent instrument to promote Christian education. In Roman lands, this Christian view of parental authority and responsibility to imparting Christian education, was accepted without question. The family imparted not only Christian education, but also prepared the child for the membership of Church. Finally he was baptised and accepted by the Holy Church.

By the early sixth century the authority of the Christian Church became known to all, but it had to face many sorts of difficulties. In order to propagate its religious teachings, the Church needed its own schools where a formal schooling system could be operated.

But the majority of the early Christians looked at the Roman Culture and education with suspicion and rejected their intellectual conventions. In the beginning, they often rejected and sometimes accepted the pagan literature, which contained grammar teaching and rhetorical accomplishments. But a total rejection of the existing schooling system was quite impossible. Although the Christians lacked pagan practices and beliefs, they had to accept the value of grammar and rhetoric. Thus the early Christian schools, blended with the Christian tidings and pagan grammar and rhetoric teaching, came into existence.

A few of the best representatives of the Christian position, during the fourth to the fifth century, were St. Augustine, St. Ambrose and St. Jerome, who believed that pagan learning and the forming of the Christian character were complementary and could go hand in hand. In his *Of Christian Doctrine* St. Augustine praised the liberal arts and expressed to combine them with theology. A further closer correspondence between learning the Christian truth in pagan schools was expressed by St. Jerome, who saw the classics and their literary implements as necessary instruments for Christians. He plainly accepted that truth is truth wherever it is found. Such expressions made by the Church Apostles or Fathers showed that a liberal attitude existed towards the pagan schools. This led the children of Christians to attend the pagan schools where they began with letters, reading and writing and went beyond to continue with the study of grammar and literature. As a result of the existing liberal attitude and encouragement towards education, in a few years there were not only a great number of Christian students but teachers also who could teach at all educational levels.

The question, 'Who laid the foundation of the Christian educational tradition?' is rather complex. Some historians believe that it was Christ Himself who started such a tradition. While the others give this credit to His apostles, who through their writings gave birth to such traditions. In fact, Christ and His disciples were revolutionaries who directed their teaching at the salvation of souls and up-held 'justice' against the old law. They started with 'charity'. Thus, these fundamental doctrines were instrumental to form Christian educational views which were elaborated by the Church apostles. Some of the early Christians who were mainly responsible for shaping the Christian educational traditions were Clement of Alexandria (ca. 150-215 A.D.), Origen (ca. 185-254), Jerome (331-420), and Augustine (354-430).[1]

Clement of Alexandria was one of the first Christian thinkers to be really aware of a theory of education. Although his contemporaries took him to be a 'liberal Christian' but his liberalism was not offensive and for many centuries he was called a saint.

Clemant became famous as a teacher. His institution, a Catchetical school', was like the Academy of Plato. It was like a good home, consisting of an excellent library which was liked by the youth of Alexandria. In this school, he taught Christian doctrines and discussed on the Scriptures. His work was greatly admired by the authorities of the Christian Church of that time.

His three works, *Protreptikos*, *Paidagogos* and *Stromateis* contain his theory of education which reflects his Christian theological ideals and practices. In *Paidagogos* he is more concerned with the character formation of youth. The theme of morality has been discussed at a great length, as for him the inculcation of virtue is more important than knowledge.

Paidagogos is immediately of interest because of its title. *Paidagogos*, meaning the attendant, describes how the attendant waited upon the child and accompanied to and from the various places of instruction. In *Paidagogos* Christ is presented as the teacher of humanity, not as a professor cultivating intellect and mental skills, but as a model in whom men could find example.[2]

Origen was appointed as the head of Clement's school at Alexandria by the bishop Demetrius in A.D. 204. Origen is reported to be of eighteen years when he was given the charge of the Catechtical school. He soon came to prominence as he tried to break off the teaching of secular letters thinking that was opposed to sacred study. Origen reversed his position and came to realize that religious knowledge proceeded best on a foundation of formal studies, and he enlarged the school to include a full classical programme.[3]

Origen left Alexandria around the year A.D. 216 due to the persecution of Christians in that city by the emperor Caracalla. After travelling to many countries he returned to Caesarea on the Palestine cost in A.D. 231. There he was received enthusiastically. It was here in Caesarea that he established a school and passed the remaining years of life there.

Origen from the beginning was greatly influenced by Clement. He saw, like his master, that wisdom comes only from God and the first step towards knowledge lies in accepting the importance of faith. Words may give sometimes the appearance of knowledge but the knowledge of the highest good which cannot at all be expressed in words.[4]

He further reflected that he was greatly anxious that all men should devote their strength to Christianity for achieving the right end. He said that man is comprised of free will and ignorance, which should be transformed through discipline and cultivation and that 'a Christian has a positive duty to encourage men to be wise'.[5]

Origen's concepts were very lucid and he acknowledged that education was the way to virtue and the spiritual growth (attainment of virtue) was the goal of man.

St. Jerome's *Vulgate* and *Lives of Great Men* contain enough evidence that he was a great scholar.

Jerome possessed great powers of diligency and had a wide learning. He knew Latin, Greek and Hebrew equally well. He contributed to all topics—'ecclesiastical, history, apologetics, exegesis, scriptures'[6] and made commentaries, biblical translations and wrote letters as well.

He was born in the western Latin-speaking province of Dalmatia in the city of Stridon. His parents were Christians. He completed his early education under the great grammarian Aclius Donatus who lived in Rome.

It was in Rome that Jerome finally became committed to the scholarly life by accepting a papal commission to prepare a Latin translation of the Psalms and the New Testament from the original Hebrew and Greek.[7] Besides, he wrote several minor works between A.D. 374 to 379. His biblical translations were his first major work and his life's greatest achievement.

His writings are greatly biased by Christian ideals and he very often reflects his distaste towards secular books and their study. Reporting one of his dreams, 'Lord if ever I possess or read secular books again I will be guilty of denying you': he shows his disbelief in the study of the pagan literature and reflects a great enthusiasm towards the Christian faith.

In his various works Jerome's 'main theme is fear of the Lord'. The soul must be educated as the temple of God and so the child must neither hear nor say anything except that which pertains to the fear of god.[8]

In one of his letters, Jerome unfolded his belief in the principles of negativism and withdrawal of the child from the multitude to save him from immorality.

He would want even the attendants themselves aloof from the world, and the teacher to be of mature age, having a blameless character and scholarly achievement. Perhaps, Rousseau was very much influenced by Jerome's negativism which he re-stressed in his *Emile* in the eighteenth century.

Jerome also had a plan for the training of the beginners when they learnt letters of alphabets. He suggested that letters should be cut out in ivory or boxwood shapes for the child to handle and to trace out them with his fingers. Some of these ideas were adopted by Montessori for teaching alphabets to children in her school many centuries after him.

St. Augustine was born in the North African city of Tagaste. His father was a pagan and mother a Christian.[9] During his early years he went to a grammar school at Madauna, a place twenty miles away from his birth place. At the age of seventeen he was sent to a school of rhetoric, where he stayed for three years. When his studies were completed he became a teacher of rhetoric.

In 385 A.D., he went to Milan to take up an appointment as professor of rhetoric. A year after this, he achieved his conversion which he mainly sought after reading the *Life of Anthony* and Platonic philosophy and literature. He returned to Tagaste and was ordained priest at Hippo and succeeded to the bishop's chair in 396 A.D.

One of his important books, *Confessions* was published in 397 A.D. It contains his most important ideas about the reality of God and the divinity of Christ, which are very often reflected in the book.

Augustine's metaphysical concepts are borrowed from Plato, more specially the belief in the fundamental duality about the existence of the two worlds—man's earthly tenure and God's eternal kingdom, similar to Plato's realms of Becoming and Being.

In the opening sentences of the *Confessions* Augustine reflects: 'Our hearts are restless until they find peace in you. Man's vocation is to get the union with Him. The search for peace is a lifelong process of man.'[10]

In his *De Magistro (*On the Teacher*)* and *De Doctrine Christiana* (On Christian Education) published in A.D. 389 and 426 respectively, he directed his thoughts to the theory of education and important epistemological questions like, what is knowledge and where from does it come? What part does man's reason play towards that knowledge? And how can man achieve ultimate knowledge?

Augustine believed that truth is pre-existent, yet latent and man's task is to make the latent manifest.[11] To him learning was that process which would bring consciousness of clarity to the obscure and unconscious ideas. Recognizing the importance of reason in man, he reflected that it should be developed to help man grow spiritually. He said that reason was a very useful agent which was responsible for bringing awareness of the external world and could direct man towards God.

Reflecting about the teacher, he upheld that a teacher should be versed in the skills of the liberal arts, logic, rhetoric and grammar so that he could help his students to develop well. He also recommended the study of mathematics for it could develop insight into divinity and the universe.

The Fall of the Classical System

The Christian movement which had started in Rome, was spread beyond it by the missionaries. They carried the gospel of Christ far and wide and by the time of Constantine's reign (306-337 AD) its strength became remarkable. Constantine decreed in Milan (313 AD.) to stop the persecution of Christians and at the same time showed great interest in education. The decree led to the opening of schools on all levels and almost everywhere in his Empire. Constantine encouraged schools and rewarded the missionaries generously for their work. It was this time that Christian teachers in even greater number than before found their way into the schools. Thus due to lack of proper patronage for the classical schools and due to the growth of the monastic schools under Constantine's Empire, the classical school system began to decline.

The newly created Christian schools, mainly monastic schools, had a few problems in the beginning. There was no proper curriculum and not many pupils to whom such schools would impart teaching, but by the Middle Ages there developed a fairly definite theory of Christian education. The Christians were now quite certain what schools ought to teach. But to reach this stage of educational evolution, great efforts were made by some Christian missionaries who were religious men and good teachers as well.

Boethius (ca 480-525) was one of the ancient Christians who was also known as the first of the Scholastics, who helped shaping the Christian intellectual traditions. His great work *Consolation of Philosophy*, a popular textbook of the middle Ages, must have been read by all at that time. Besides *Consolation* he wrote some pastoral poetry, prepared an arithmetic book based on the earlier work of Nichomachus and translated works of Plato and Aristotle. Boethius offered, in addition to writing on philosophy and education, treatises on theology and music and many commentaries on the works of classical authors. He was a great inspiration to the Christians. He integrated much of classical learning and pagan doctrines with a healthy but orthodox Christian faith. He led the early Middle Ages to the door steps of philosophy, and laid down the foundations of the budding Christian intellect and philosophy.[12]

St. Benedict (ca 480-546) was born of rich parents at Nursia near Rome. Perhaps in his sixteenth year after attending some school in Rome, Benedict renounced the worldly life and retired to a cave near Subiaco about forty miles away from Rome, where he followed the most vigorous ascetic practices.[13]

Benedict gradually founded some monasteries and provided guidance to the monks and similar institutions. In the year 529 he founded a new monastery on Monte Cassino.

Benedict's *Rule*, which was greatly influenced by Jerome's Latin translation of Pachomius's *Rule*, contains the regulations and a code of conduct for the monks to live a disciplined life in the monasteries. The monastery was supposed to be self-sufficient and internally consistent, providing a completed way of life for the monks. The monks would elect an abbot who contained all authority in him and was considered accountable for his flock at the day of judgment. The abbot was also responsible for their salvation.[14]

The rules contained in the *Rule* were prescribed mainly for the monks of Monte Cassino, where activities of learning too, received attention, but less consideration was paid to the scholarly and intellectual endeavour. Gradually the *Rule* became quite popular and was modestly adopted by the existing monasteries mainly in Italy. The type of monasteries that Benedict founded and the rules he prescribed became the principal agency for preservation and advancement of learning and culture during the period from the sixth to the twelth century.[15]

Flavius Magnus Aurelius Cassiodorus Senator (ca. 480-575) was born of a wealthy family in south Italy. After being educated in rhetoric and philosophy Cassiodorus began his public life as an assessor.[16]

While still in public service, Cassiodorus wrote a *Chronicon*, an abstract history of the world, and the *Gothic History* in twelve books. Besides writing these books he also wrote both public and personal letters which showed his unusual historical sense and insight.

His religious outlook was first displayed in *On the Soul* having twelve books.

Cassiodorus plans to establish a theological school in Rome did not succeed but he founded two monasteries on his own ancestral estate, having scriptural study as their chief objective. In these monasteries, writing and study were regular and important parts of the discipline of the monastery. There was a place known as the Scriptorium in the monasteries, where monks copied the scriptures and the writing of Fathers. The Scriptorium was well organised and enabled monks to support themselves by preparing manuscripts.[17]

Cassiodorus had a liberal attitude towards the study of the liberal arts, for like St. Augustine, he thought that the arts were simply aids to the study of theology.

In his Introduction to *Divine and Human Reading* Cassiodorus unfolded an educational syllabus for the intellectually inclined monks.

Some important contributions of Cassiodorus were to make the monks to copy manuscripts and transforming the monastery into a theological school. His *Divine and Human Reading* contained the outline for the seven liberal arts (grammar, rhetoric, dialectic, arithmetic, geometry, music and astronomy), and was treated as one of the important school books of the early Middle Ages. His two monasteries performed the function of preserving early medieval culture as the encouraged monks collected selections of the Church Fathers and kept them in their libraries. Above all, Cassiodorus kept the linguistic discipline alive and put it within a Christian theoretical educational frame-work.[18]

Gregory the Great's (540-604) education was comprised of the secular as well as the divine arts. Since he was a monk and was a political officer who was in a position of education he was bound to make a great impression on Christians.

Gregory was very much interested in the administration, discipline, education and administration of the Church. But he was a practical person so he wanted Christian education to be practised by the followers of Christianity. This education included home training and moral formation at the most elementary levels. He very much approved of the monastic schools' plans and practices and endorsed most of Benedict's proposals.

Christian Education in Ireland

With the decline of the Roman Empire, the old classical schools gradually became in disuse and learning seemed to have reached its lowest ebb in the Continent for three to four centuries. But Ireland had a different story. Learning was enjoyed very well there.

Since Ireland was not a part of the Roman Empire, its education was not affected either by the rise or the fall of the Empire. Though it is difficult to estimate the type or the extent of education and culture existing in Ireland during pre-Christian times, there seem to have been Celtic scholars who conducted schools and Celtic literature there at the time. A good evidence of Irish Culture and tradition, teachers, schools and written literature existed in Ireland before the Christian scholars and education migrated there from the Continent.[19]

It was the monastic schools system (600 century) which first came into existence in Ireland, but Irish monasticism and Irish monastic schools were somewhat different from their Continental counterparts. The chief features of the monastic education which contained the Christian traditions for more than two centuries were as follows:[20]

(i) As the monastic schools grew in number, the Irish bardic schools, which were mostly run by laymen, collapsed. But in want of Latin literature and grammar in Ireland at that time, the Christian teachers had to rely on classics.

(ii) The monastic schools provided mainly the elementary and secondary education which was deemed to be important for the formation of character of the individual. Although it is not clearly known what kind of education was given to the girls, they were provided opportunities to educate themselves. Foreign students were also welcomed to these schools.

(iii) Besides teaching of science without experimental and observational techniques, the seven liberal arts and religions were also taught in the Irish monastic schools.

(iv) The monasteries supported these schools which were noted for their literary activities. Each of these schools possessed a scriptorium and a library. Thus, the culture and education which had been imported to Ireland during the sixth century was transmitted to the Continent by the Irish monks and scholars with greater fervour and intensity during the eighth century.

Further Decline of the Ancient Culture

It is said that Continental Europe had a dark period of culture and education for nearly three hundred years after the sixth century. Partly it could be true as the ancient education was at the lowest ebb in the Continent at the time of the decline of the Roman Empire. But all was not that bad. The monasteries which had originated in the Empire had spread to Ireland and many countries of the Continent had already accepted the monastic system of education. Besides, the Moselem learning which contained the religious doctrines of **Mohammed** (569-632), contained in the Holy Koran, became popular in the Continent during the early 9th century.

The Arabic language and the religious doctrines, including music, science, architecture, literature and philosophy were the various ingredients of the Arabic culture which was picked up by the Mohammedans when they moved their victorious armies from West of Arabia to northern Africa and Spain. These religious crusaders took the philosophy and science of the Greeks, borrowed ideas, specially from India . China, and mixed them with their own ideas. These Moslems or Mohammedans were selective but did not reject anything of the alien culture which they thought good.[21]

They not only introduced some of the Greek literature and Arabic notation but invented algebra too.

They were very skilful and imaginative in the practical arts. The manufacture of paper goes to their credit. Although they learnt this art from the Chinese, it was tremendously perfected by them. It led to the progress of learning and cultural growth in the coming centuries.

One more important influence of the Moslems is noteworthy. Since they were creative, they displayed it in the field of theology. It posed a challenge to the Christianity. As a result the Christian theologians perfected their own system. Thus the Moslem threat resulted in bringing up real Christian theological scholarship and the Christian University of the medieval period. The Greek culture had already reached the lowest ebb by then.

Revival of Learning

The first wave of the revival of learning or the Renaissance was witnessed on the Continent in the beginning of the ninth century. The main sources, which stepped up the first revival of learning, were the growth of monasticism, spread of education in Ireland and the growth of Moslem culture and education. With these three potent forces crystallizing the revival, names of **Charlemagne** (Charles the Great: 768-814) and his chief education adviser, **Alcuin,** need to be included. Efforts of Charlemagne and Alcuin were indispensable and resulted in culminating the revival of learning.

Education, for the first time, received royal patronage in the court of Charles the Great. This made the other princess of other countries accept the importance of education. They too provided patronage to it. Chivalrous princes seemed to be more eager to spread it in their boundaries. Education and knighthood went hand in hand for a long time during the ninth to eleventh centuries, but education of women received less attention in the ninth century. It ended with domestic training for both ordinary and unusual women.

Charles the Great as a leader of rare qualities, was a great organiser, a good administrator and possessed with humanitarian instincts.[22] When the year 800 ended, he became successor to the ancient Roman emperors of the West and was recognised as the ruler of the Continental German-Roman World. Since he was a very powerful ruler, peace was restored in his empire. This brought the easy growth of education in his domain. Besides, Charles himself took an active interest in education of children and demanded better education for the clergy. It helped literary advancement in the Church too.

One of his biographers, Einhard, reports Charlemagne's interest in the following lines:[23]

> "The Plan that he adopted for his children's education was, first of all, to have both boys and girls instructed in the liberal arts, to which he also turned his own attention"...

And when they have learned the liberal arts, "the boys had to learn horsemanship, and to practise war and the chase, and the girls to familiarise themselves with cloth making, and to handle the distaff and spindle, that they might not grow indolent through idleness, and foster in them every virtuous sentiment".

Charles was not only the patron but a student as well. He encouraged the scholars of his court which brought good literary output. Besides, he issued edicts and decrees, including letters of advice which helped in promoting education. One of his edicts issued in 802 had have a great effect on bringing about a revival of general learning. The edict having the imperial authority directed Parish priests to instruct children in the elements of learning. It contained:[24]

> "Let the priests keep schools in the villages and towns, and if any of the faithful wish to give his little ones to learning they ought willingly to receive them and teach them gratuitously, remembering what has been written".

It continued further: "And let them (priests) exact no price from the children for their teaching, nor receive anything from them save what the parents may offer voluntarily and from affection".

Such efforts were bound to accelerate and revive learning. These efforts were furthered by Alcuin, who first was appointed by Charles the schoolmaster of the palace school.

ALCUIN (ca. 735-804) obtained his early education a the Cathedral school of York. He remained at York as a student and a teacher until 782 when he became the master of the palace school at Aachen. The palace school was already in operation for seven years before Alcuin joined it. Alcuin up-lifted the reputation of the school and soon it was known as an intellectual centre. During his fourteenth years' of stay in the royal patronage, Alcuin made tremendous contributions to education. Some of them are listed here under.[25]

(i) He recognised that a competent elementary education was a first, and necessary, step towards educational reforms.

(ii) He devised an elementary syllabus and a pedagogy for teaching Latin and other practical subjects.

(iii) He prepared Latin grammar textbooks to enable students to learn an accurate, functional Latin.

(iv) He improved elementary teaching, popularised it and developed techniques for attaining greater teaching efficiency.

(v) He encouraged the cultivation of a closer relationship between liberal learning and spiritual knowledge.

(vi) He also wrote a number of worthwhile books on education which affected the educational consciousness of his age.

Alcuin is not a writer of original books, but he was an able compiler and a literal transcriber of the works of others. He is reckoned as the great man of his times because he correctly assessed the current and imperative needs of education and selected a pedagogy for the school, which aimed at fundamental goals of learning. Some of his books, *On the Virtues and Vices, On the Nature of the Soul, and On Grammar and On Rhetoric and the Virtues*, are great contributions in the fields of theology and teaching techniques. Alcuin is the one who rarely reflected on the Christian theory of learning and recommended the study of the seven arts, which he thought necessary to boost up higher wisdom.[26]

Thus, by the end of the tenth century not only the remaining fragments of the Roman Empire collapsed to a point of almost nothingness, its original classical schools system also decayed to a great extent, except that during the sixth century the growth of the Christian monastic schools brought back some of the classical elements in their system to retain linguistic competencies. The educational growth, during the so called Dark Ages was not prominent but Ireland had its own contribution towards a modern culture even at that time. The rapid growth of the monastic system backed by Boethius's and Cassiodorus's efforts and writings, the growth of education in Ireland and royal patronage given to education during the reign of Charlemagne, brought a new wave of learning to the Continent. It paved the way for the greater revival of learning or the Renaissance which flourished on the Continent from thirteenth and fourteenth centuries onwards.

REFERENCES

1. Power, *History of Education*, p. 211.
2. Bowen, *History of Western Education*, p. 241.
3. Bowen, *History of Western Education*, p. 246.
4. Origen (tr. 1957), *Contra, Celsum*, translated by Henry Chadwick, (Cambridge: Cambridge University Press), pp. VI, III, 3.
5. Origen, *Contra-Celsum*, pp. III, XI, IV.
6. Power, *History of Education*, p. 226.
7. Power, *History of Education*, p. 227.
8. Jerome, *E.P.: AD Laetam De institutione filiage*, IV.
9. Bowen, *History of Western Education*, p. 271.

10. Augustine, *Confessionum* I.
11. Bowen, *History of Western Education*, p. 279.
12. Power, *History of Education*, pp. 249-51.
13. Bowen, *History of Western Education*, p. 331.
14. Chadwick O. (1958), *Western Asceticism: Selected Translations* (London: SCM Press) pp. Intr. pp. 20-25.
15. Power, *History of Education*, p. 253.
16. Power Edward J. (1959), *Evolution of Educational Doctrine* (New York. Appleton-Century Inc.), p. 137.
17. Power, *History of Education*, pp. 255-57.
18. Power, *History of Education*, pp. 258-62.
19. James J. Auchmuty (1937), *Irish Education*, Dublin: Hodges, Figgs & Co., pp. 6-20.
20. Power, *History of Education*, pp. 268-71.
21. Power, *History of Education*, pp. 271-73.
22. Woodruft Douglas (1934), *Charlemagne*, (London: P. Davies Ltd.), pp. 140-43.
23. Einhard (1960), *Life of Charlemagne*, (University of Michigan: Ann Arbor) pp. 3-70.
24. Quoted in Patrick J. MeCormick & Francis P. Cassidy (1953), *History of Education* (Washington D.C.: The Catholic Education Press), p. 222.
25. Power, *History of Education*, pp. 279-80.
26. Seven Liberal Arts: Grammar, Rhetoric, Dialectic, Arithmetic, Geometry, Music and Astronomy.

CHAPTER-IV

THE GROWTH OF MEDIEVAL EDUCATION

Soon after Charlemagne's death, for want of a strong ruler, his Empire started disintegrating and gradually different nations emerged out of it. The history of Europe during the tenth century witnessed much disorder. It was at this time that the threats from the attacks of the Norsemen, the Moors and the Magyars also grew. It was only the beginning of the eleventh century, when the European world of learning began to wear a new face.[1]

It was the beginning of the Renaissance too. The Renaissance movement was a gradual one. As it advanced to the various parts of the Continent, it started affecting physical, cultural, social and political aspects of the countries. By the end of the eleventh century and beginning of the twelfth century, quite a strong wave of the revival of learning swept the most part of the Continent.

The medieval educational awakening, backed by the fully established Irish monastic system and the royal patronage enjoyed in the recent past, instrumented a variety of schools. Though some of these kinds of schools had been inherited from the past, many others were invented to fill special needs of the times.[2]

Schools in the Medieval Period

One of the sorts of schools, which the medieval age witnessed, were the *monastic schools*. The impetus for their development came largely from the laws of the Church and royal decrees issued by Charlemagne. Despite their natural antagonism towards the classical learning, the monasteries had to accept certain literary features of the classical learning. Gradually the monasteries and their schools assumed a certain scholastic character which laid the foundation of the medieval monastic schools.

The medieval monastic schools had regular teachers, some of whom were monks. They had a fairly broad course of studies which included the seven liberal arts.[3] Some progressive monastic schools also had professional curricula of law and medicine.

Grammar was one of the important subjects of the medieval schools-curriculum. By studying grammar, a student would learn how to write good Latin. According to Alcuin, Latin grammar was helpful in boosting up reason. It was also taken to be a divine language and so it was needed to be studied. The monastic teachers had Donatus and Priscian as the best sources and authority on grammar in the medieval period. So, after the study of such authorised grammarians, students went on to literature. They studied the Latin classics. Virgil and the other Christian writers were recommended for study by the monastic authorities, but the Greek classics were not popular at that time.

Besides grammar, study of logic was welcomed by the monastic schools. Boethius' translation of *Categories* and Aristotle's *De Interpretatione* were the main sources of the study of logic. Next to logic was the study of rhetoric. Cicero's and Quintilian's rhetorical works were very much liked for the study of rhetoric then.

Since the introduction of the Arabic notations, arithmetic had undergone big changes. The monastic schools accepted the study of the updated arithmetic along with geometry and astronomy which had practical utility. By the medieval times the study of both the theory and practice of advanced music had been accepted. The monastic schools prepared solemn and spiritually oriented harmonies. Medieval time witnessed highly developed courses in music which were implemented in the monastic schools.

There is not much proof that the Church supported education but the schools related to the Church played important roles and advanced education to a great extent. By the eleventh century, England had been showing much interest in education and the ecclesiastical laws of England had taken stands in support of better educational opportunities. The Church legislation required priests and clergymen to direct the training of young men in the manual arts and crafts. Gradually the Church's educational policy was born and educational opportunities to all, who wanted to study secular subjects, were extended. This resulted in opening of new educational institutions in Europe. The Church schools started playing more important roles in European education for many centuries to come. Some of the important educational institutions of the medieval period are described here under.

Cathedral Schools

From the twelfth to the fifteenth century the cathedral schools played quite an important role in spreading educational opportunities in Europe. There were great numbers of cathedral churches to which schools were attached. Many priests were assigned to these churches. The priests were organised into chapters and lived under a canon (rule), so they were called *Canons*. Each chapter (college) also had a dean who would be superior to a canon. Besides the dean, there was a cleric in charge of music, a treasurer and schoolmaster known as a chancellor. The chancellor had a general supervisory function over all sorts of educational involvements in the cathedral. There were also great churches besides the cathedrals. These great churches had chapters assigned to canons who would also teach there.

The curricula of these cathedral schools differed widely depending on the chapter's cleric talent for teaching. Some schools imparted only elementary teaching while others taught the seven arts and led their pupils to higher learning.

There were also bigger cathedrals which had schools with almost complete curricula having theological courses, arithmetic, geometry, music and astronomy. Some big cathedral schools offered divinity courses leading to clerical ordination. The smaller cathedral schools taught grammar, rhetoric and logic. Some of these were meant to impart training in music and songs only and trained the boys for church choirs.

Court Schools

If cathedral schools provided a foundation in which universities could be built, the court schools (Palace Schools) shared some of the responsibility for education and provided a higher quality of educational opportunity. The court schools, being secular in outlook, retained much of medieval intellectual life.

In fact, court schools were old institutions which also existed in the 9th century so the clerks were needed by the royal courts. One of the functions of such a school was to train the clerks for the court-jobs. Besides, nobles also sought to improve their minds through literature. So they utilised the court schools to learn the fundamental literary skills. The larger, wealthier courts usually had greater resources and founded good court schools. Mostly, these court schools provided elementary education for noble children and trained clerks and other civil servants.[4] Thus, the court schools had a limited number of pupils and had a select clientele. In the great court schools advanced curricula were sometimes organised and medicine, theology and science were taught. Henry II, King of England had a good court school which existed between 1154 to 1189.[5]

The court schools also provided the type of education needed for knights. It was the dawn of the age of chivalry and the knights were the important public figures, who provided the overlords the needed military power. So to lead young men to knighthood by providing a regular training programme, was one of the tasks of a court school.

An ideal knight was commissioned to protect the church and to fight against treachery. He fought to defend the poor and tried to bring peace in his own area or land. The knights were educated men who were more chivalrous than philosophers, therefore, they did not exert much influence on medieval intellectual culture. The court schools must be given due credit for the training of these medieval knights.

Municipal Schools

A variety of schools were established under municipal auspices. These town schools, as they were called then, had a big support from the common people as they were the people who got most benefit from them. There were Latin grammar schools (secondary schools), which were intended mainly for the sons of merchants and shopkeepers. These Latin schools were patterned after the church schools as methods of instruction and curriculum were concerned. There were town schools, where the common people could learn to read and write. Since all could not reach the grammar schools, the town schools became quite popular as these provided instruction in reading and writing in the vernacular and offered the elements of learning to all who wanted them. There were parish schools which also provided elementary teaching and were dependent almost entirely on the goodwill of the pastor. But the parish schools were never fully taken to be public schools, so the town schools were regarded as supplements to parish education.

The town schools and all the municipal schools undoubtedly contributed to the growth of education and heightened the interest in education. As very often, there existed tension between the town schools and the church schools, it also helped increasing the educational quality. More educational opportunity increased as a result of the growth of the municipal schools during the medieval period and historians believe that the municipal schools were the forerunners of the medieval universities.

Guild Schools

Guilds were mainly the associations of persons who joined hands to protect their common interests. In the medieval times there were different kinds of guilds, such as guilds of teachers and students and guilds that were established by craftsmen and merchants. But not all such guilds were indifferent to providing educational training. Every guild was vitally concerned with education in a broad sense. Each guild prescribed the steps involved and supervised the quality of training. The guilds that were formed among craftsmen and merchants kept their aim of producing good merchants and craftsmen and in doing so they not only protected their own réputation but also safeguarded the public interest.

Very often the guild was responsible for extending educational opportunity for the children of guild members. So the guilds created schools which were of elementary types and employed schoolmasters to run the schools. There was yet another way in which a guild very often associated with education. Without having a direct control on schools, the guilds contributed generously towards their support. The guilds' greatest significance lay in the fact that through them the opportunities for education in the medieval years were considerably broadened.[6]

Thus, the variety of schools, which flourished during the medieval period, created 'a medieval scholarly world' quite aware of the classical authors and classical knowledge. It was the beginning of the scholastic period.

The Dawn of Scholasticism

With the dawn of the twelfth century, Scholasticism started coming over the horizon of the medieval Christian world. It was a great intellectual movement, made mainly by the medieval Christians to integrate the medieval Christian values and newly discovered classical material. Scholasticism lasted for about two centuries. During this period it was quite dominant and greatly human. Though it could not much affect the lives of the people, it did have some lasting impression on education.[7]

Starting with classical knowledge, Scholasticism tried to organise whole of human knowledge under the spiritual banner. So far, before the advent of Christianity, personal ambitions were judged of paramount value. 'Man is the measure of all things' was the philosophical ambition of the classical authors. Christianity would not agree to it. Christian values directed men to live outside themselves—to replace personal ambition with sacrifice and altruism. The Christian world would not be the old pagan world all over again, but would represent a distinct and a new intellectual climate.

Yet all was not that bad with the old classics. There were certain elements in the classical culture which could not be rejected. Therefore, after discarding the unwanted elements, the useful ones were retained from it. This was the same technique which St. Augustine, the early Christian philosopher, had suggested. But the twelfth century scholasticism did not wholly agree to sort out the good from the classical culture in the manner Augustine had suggested.

The new technique of purification depended on logic. Scholastics employed all the principles of logic to make reason and to retain the teachings of the church. In some fields of logic by employing dialectic, they could formulate a philosophy which was consistent with the Christian theological doctrine.[8]

But in the broad field of literature, the task of logic was more complicated. Christians would not approve of the literary references to the gods and to sensual love which were quite different to their morality. Therefore, with the help of logic, they accepted that interpretation of the texts which would render them the material that would fall within the vicinity of Christian moral teaching. Thus, by applying more scientific ways (logic) abundant classical literature was accepted by the scholastics. One of the foremost scholastics, who employed this technique, was Hugh of St. Victor. He involved the employment of logic in interpreting the inner meaning of a text. When this technique was used faultlessly, nothing in the classical literature could be judged anti-Christian.[9]

Next to literature, Scholastics turned to grammar. The application of logic to grammar was aimed to introduce dialectic to it. Traditionally, grammatical rules were framed by studying the best authors. But the scholastics changed the traditional way and asked the students to follow a grammar which could be constructed by reason. One of the important scholastics, who followed this rule and who is known as the inventor of dialectical grammar, was Alexander of Villedieu who wrote his famous *Doctrinale*.

In the field of rhetoric, Scholasticism focused on supplying a technical vocabulary for theology and philosophy but it was not necessary that the scholar paid much attention to the pagan rhetoric rules to bring out the technical vocabulary. He was forced to assert his intellectual independence and create his own style, but he could use the old rules of rhetoric too, if he chose so.

With all this new approach towards human knowledge, grammar, theology and rhetoric, Scholasticism could not summarily ignore the classical wealth of knowledge in the fields of law, medicine and literature. Many scholastic scholars re-organised and applied the ancient philosophy and knowledge of law and medicine during the medieval times, but efforts seemed to have been slow in these directions. So the new products were delayed. Despite this delay, the scholastics moved rapidly towards philosophical synthesis which became the most permanent feature of Scholasticism. Some of the scholastic philosophers, who are reckoned to be the principal exponents of scholastic philosophy, are worth mentioning here.

Peter Abelard (1079-1142)

Peter Abelard is known to be one of the most famous teachers of the medieval age. He attracted students from all over Europe and thought deeply about the question of universals. Abelard's method of dealing with the philosophical questions contained in his famous *Sic et Non* (Yes/No) influenced most of the medieval scholars. Abelard's greatest achievement in the history of thought and education was the emphasis that he put on reason as the source to reach truth.

Though Abelard had little reputation as a theologian, his approach to theological questions (by applying reason) gained him much eminence during the twelfth and the thirteenth centuries. His reputation as a teacher was great enough to promote love for higher education.

Albert the Great (1193-1280)

Albert was a famous philosopher and educationist. He used the philosophy of Aristotle as a foundation for his own philosophical thought. He was the teacher of the well known Thomas Aquinas and excelled in the fields of botany and geography. He was one of the few medieval teachers, who prepared books for the use of schools. He wrote practical books and manuals which were used by the medieval schools for a long time.

St. Thomas Aquinas (1125-1274)

Thomas Aquinas was educated by the Benedictines at their famous Italian monastery, Monte Cassino, and at the University of Paris. Albert the Great taught him at the University of Paris. Later on Aquinas taught at the University of Paris too. As a teacher he shaped the minds and influenced the thoughts of his students. Because of the permanent influence of his work and philosophy, he is still known to be a great medieval teacher.

Besides, the so-called Thomastic Philosophy is the official philosophy of the Catholic Church.

St. Thomas' impact on Christian education and thought was colossal. He maintained, like Abelard, that reason was a means for attaining truth. In his *De Magistro* (The Teacher), he discussed the importance of the teacher along with the student, the principal agent in the process.

In fact, St. Thomas' contributions as a scholar are.much more than as a good teacher. He did not provide a new educational theory but he improved upon the prevailing one. He sharpened it at certain points.

St. Thomas framed the pattern for philosophical studies. His established pattern was generally accepted for centuries. Catholic philosophers still consider his philosophic innovations valid. His approach to discover truth through reason established a permanent scholastic technique for arriving at truth.

St. Thomas' philosophy has still a privileged position in all Catholic colleges and universities as well as in ecclesiastical institutions.[10]

Educational Theory During Medieval Times

Ancient educators contributed a great deal to the growth of medieval educational theory but in spite of a few points which were in common with both, the medieval educational practice and theory, it differed from that of the ancient.

Medieval education was intended chiefly for clerics, whereas the ancient education did not know any priesthood and had set its objectives to educate the common men. There was another important difference between the medieval and the ancient education. The ancient educational theory was designed to educate citizens of this world. The medieval educational theory and practice were meant for the other world. The middle ages had definitely emphasized the education of clerics. Most of the works of the medieval scholars were concerned with the education of clergymen. Chief among them were the works of Cassiodorus, Isidore, Rabanus Mauras, Hugh of St. Victor and John of Salisbury. All of these authors were pointing towards one direction—the training of the clergymen.

For three hundred years Cassiodorus' *Introduction* remained as a charter for medieval learning. It contained the basic elements necessary for the construction of a theory of education. It dealt with the questions of *why education was necessary*, who was to be educated and what means were to be used in the process of education. Though the *Introduction* was not original, it contained a Christian tradition in learning, which continued throughout the medieval years. All this happened during the sixth century. Isidore, the archbishop of Seville, came to be known to the Christian world during the seventh century. His most important book, *Etymologies*, was a sort of work which contained much about the universal knowledge. In *Etymologies*, he discussed the seven liberal arts and their usefulness in advancing the cause of divine learning. Isidore followed the same line which Cassiodorus had maintained as far as the theory of education was concerned.

Rabanus Maurus had studied under Alcuin, who taught him that the seven liberal arts were not only useful for divine-study, but were indispensable.

In his work *On the Instruction of the Clergy,* he discussed secular learning and divine learning separately. He was quite liberal in his outlook, which may be seen in his view that grammar should include literature. So far, grammar had been studied separately from life and language.

Rabanus reflected that music should be appreciated for its importance to life as well as its proper use in church services. He approved logic as an instrument to be used in the search for truth and regarded both arithmetic and geometry as important for human knowledge. Because of such important reflections, Rabanus dominated the educational thinking of central Europe from the ninth to the twelfth centuries.[11]

It was long before the end of the twelfth century that the works of Cassiodorus, Isidore and Rabanus had greatly affected the educational thought in the medieval Christian world. Now the scholars were ready to speculate about education. From this time onwards, it became possible to speak and think in a proper sense of educational theory. During the twelfth century only a few more important works on educational theory came into light. These works were written by Hugh of St. Victor, Conrad of Hirschan and John of Salisbury.

Hugh of St. Victor wrote a prospectus, *The Pursuit of Learning*, for the education of clerics. *The Pursuit of Learning* consists of the division of knowledge into the secular and the divine.

Hugh tried to coordinate the various branches of knowledge and placed all organised knowledge under the heading of philosophy.

Though Hugh wrote mainly for educating clerics, he was not biased to limit the clerical education in the old fashioned way. He based it almost on reading. He believed that the classics were filled with all knowledge, and therefore, provided instructions on reading in order to understand the fundamental meaning of what the best authors had written. Hugh wanted students to know what did the author mean? What meaning did the book convey and how much would the contents fit into the totality of knowledge? Hugh emphasized that a book should be read for inner meaning and not for what the author seemed to narrate. Thus, Hugh recognised the importance of an allegory which the text might contain in it. What Hugh meant to convey was that most of the things in the classics conformed to Christian beliefs and values and proper reading of a text was the key to a correct understanding of it.[12]

Conrad of Hirschan was the other important educationist of the twelfth century. His *Dialogue on Authors* contains lists and discussions of the authors to be read in the monastic course of rhetorical and grammatical studies. The *Dialogue on Authors* is directed at the education of clerics too.

Another important educationist of the twelfth century was John of Salisbury. His famous work *Metalogicon* is a defence of logical studies. But more than defending logic, he gives additional attention to the Science-oriented quadrivium (arithmetic, geometry, music, astronomy) and distinguishes himself as an important educationist and a humanist of the medieval times.

Two more medieval authors need to be mentioned here. They are Vincent of Beauvais and Egidio Colonna, who in their writings reflected the importance of the cultivation of literary tastes and need to study natural science, ethics, economics, political science and philosophy. Both the writers said a good deal about the domestic training which girls need; for no medieval authors had discussed the education of women except these two.

The Medieval Universities

The greatest achievement of the Middle Ages is their universities. Their organisation and tradition greatly affected the intellectual development of Europe. These universities were the outcome of what was best in the medieval times. Their growth was instrumental for the twelfth century educational revival and intellectual upliftment in most parts of Europe.

Students from all over were available for a long time. It was the time when the teachers became important men. This led to the spread of a great scholastic wave all over Europe, and a new enthusiasm for logic and philosophy was being witnessed.

There were some willing men who were prepared to make great sacrifices of wealth and possessions in order to pursue knowledge. Eagar students and scholars did not stay with one teacher or even one school.

As more great teachers began to appear in the educational arena, crowds of students began to encircle them. This was the beginning of the age of the universities.

New thoughts began to pour into the intellectual climate of the universities. Constantinople, Syria, Sicily and Spain were the places which had been having more texts of the ancient sciences and philosophy than the West. Aristotle's famous works, *Physics, Metaphysics* and *On the Soul,* were now easily available to those who wanted to read them. Arabic scholars introduced Greek mathematics, medical and philosophical knowledge from all the available material and a great desire for higher learning grew in the people. This led to the growth of the medieval universities.

As a result of the Church's policy, which it had framed sometime during the eleventh century, some very famous monastic and Cathedral schools developed. After a few years these schools became the medieval universities. Students came to these schools from far and wide. Therefore, the Church also led to the growth of the medieval universities.

Besides the Church, royal patronage also affected the growth of the universities. The emperors of Germany and various kings of France established universities in their own areas.

The popularity of Scholastic philosophy and reputation of individual teachers grew hand in hand. As the facilities for learning grew, men began to attach more importance to education and a great significance was attached to the subjects which interested them. The curriculum could no longer be limited to clerical studies. The universities began to offer studies in four faculties which were arts, law, medicine and theology. Although there were few medieval universities, which offered studies in all the four faculties, all the universities did offer arts and specialised in one of the other faculties.

University Organisation and Tradition

In medieval times there were guilds of various kinds everywhere. The medieval universities, too, were formed on the same basis. There were guilds of masters or students or both. The name University, *Universita,* meant a corporate body of persons, usually a guild, and what we call a university, the *Studium generale* or simply *Studium* or *Schola,* was only one kind of *universitas.*[13]

There was a most renowned university at Paris. Many medieval universities followed the same pattern of organization which the university of Paris had. Another important university of the Middle Ages was Bologna. In fact, the Middle Ages had two different types of university organisations: The master's university, like that of Paris, and the students' university, like that of Bologna. In the university of Paris the masters controlled the education. In the latter type the students were in charge of all academic programmes and policies.[14]

In the south, at Bologna, the control of university affairs was in the hands of a student council, which determined the fee to be collected and the salaries to be paid to the professors. But in northern universities the control was in the hands of the masters.

All types of universities, whether they were controlled by students or teachers, had to receive their charters and formal legal rights from the Church or from the State. The administration of scholastic matters was done by the faculty concerned. Originally the term 'faculty' meant a subject of study, but later on it came to mean a body of professors in a given subject.[15]

The deans of the faculties, with the help of other councils, usually elected a rector, who was the head of the whole university. In the south of Europe the rector was usually a student, but in the north the rector was a professor, later on, in place of a rector, there came a Chancellor who became the real head of the university.

The chief methods of teaching, employed by teachers at the medieval universities, were lectures, repetitions and disputations. Lectures were given by masters on the subject of one of the selected texts. The repetition used to be a detailed discussion of a course of lectures that had already been given. The disputation method was one of the university's important exercises in learning. Disputation was an important and a regular university technique, which provided opportunities for clearing up difficulties which the students had in their studies. Such exercises also provided students with practice in dialectic, which meant a sort of skillful arguing.

Student life at the university was not very easy. Some students came to the university with plenty of money for themselves; others came with limited funds and had to supplement their needs by begging or by seeking scholarships. They lived in the houses that the university had approved and took meals at local taverns.

The medieval students could willingly move from one university to the other. This was the most unusual characteristic of the medieval times. There were no academic obstacles to such transfers by the students.

The medieval masters, who were called professors or doctors, were members of a teaching guild. As members of a guild, they had their say in all the policy matters and academic affairs of the guild. They were admitted to the guild, not by the rector of the university or by a faculty dean, but by the masters who were already established members.

Medieval universities played a significant role in the development of European education and culture. With the help of their well qualified teachers, they compelled the lower schools to improve their quality of work. Besides, the universities did a great service for mankind by providing educated men for the administration of human affairs and to bring social and cultural emancipation.

REFERENCES

1. Poole, R.L. (1940), *Illustrations of the History of Medieval Thought and Learning*; (New York: The MacMillan Co.), pp. 95-99.
2. Power, *History of Education*, p. 286.
3. The seven liberal arts were grammar, rhetoric, dialectic, arithmetic, geometry, music and astronomy.
4. Power, *History of Education*, pp. 294-95.
5. Davis, W.S. (1923), *Life of a Medieval Barony* (New York: Harper & Row), pp. 114-23.
6. Leach, A.F. (1915), *Schools of Medieval England* (London Methuen & Co. Ltd.) pp. 70-75.
7. Taylor, H.O. (1930), *The Medieval Mind* (New York: MacMillan Co.), pp. 150-210.
8. Hugh of St. Victor (1961), *Didascalicon: A Medieval Guide to the Arts*. Translated by Jerome Taylor; (New York: Columbia University Press), pp. III viii 90-92.
9. Power, *History of Education*, pp. 304-305.
10. Power, *History of Education*, pp. 308-309.
11. Power, *History of Education*, pp. 310-312.
12. Bolgar, R.R. (1954), *The Classical Heritage and Its Beneficiaries* (Cambridge University Press), pp. 120-125.
13. Daly Lowrie J. (1961), *The Medieval University* (New York: Sheed & Ward, Inc.,) pp. III-117.
14. Power, *History of Education*, pp. 318-19.
15. Power, *History of Education*, p. 321.

CHAPTER-V

THE ADVENT OF HUMANISM

The establishment of the medieval universities and the quickening of the intellectual movement during the twelfth century became instrumental for further cultural and educational growth during the thirteenth and the fourteenth centuries. Yet the educational theory, which was the end product of the twelfth century cultural growth, could not be accepted in totality by the thirteenth or the fourteenth century educationists. The dogmatic assumptions of the medieval age were not acceptable by the educational revival of the fourteenth century. The later movement was more humanistic and was a product of a slow cultural process, which had been going on for centuries.[1]

Humanism is often another name given to the fourteenth century revival of learning or the Renaissance. The Renaissance cannot be described very easily. It was a number of things: it was a renewal of contacts with classical Greece and Rome; it was an emphasis on humanism; it was a collecting of manuscripts, and a criticism and dissemination of their contents; in part, it was a studied disregard for the centuries that had intervened between the close of the classical period and the onset of the Renaissance (1350); and finally, it was a heightening of the spirit of individualism among men.[2]

The Renaissance movement kept closer and firmer contacts with the classical past. But, it did not preoccupy itself with the past only; it also looked forward. It looked backward for impetus; it looked forward to the time when a better life would be available to men of talents. The progress of education during such a period could, by no means, be insignificant. Both in theory and practice, the Renaissance education was revolutionary and it finally produced a theory which had not been familiar to the medieval times.[3]

Educational Theory During Renaissance Times

The medieval educational theory contained the Christian tradition in learning which was intended mainly for clerics. The theory sustaining Renaissance education reflected the changes taking place in life and society during the fourteenth century. Therefore it should have been different from the Scholastic dogmatic assumptions of the medieval age.

Being revolutionary in nature at the very outset, the Renaissance education fed itself on the classical doctrines which produced classical pedagogy. The ancient Greek and Hellenistic schools were taken to be the models and a great number of quotations and allusions were incorporated by the Renaissance authors in their works. A careful examination of the Renaissance literature reveals that the authors of that period depended rather heavily on their classical predecessors.

This kind of borrowing was not quite unconventional. The medieval educational writers also knew their classical sources. Vincent of Beauvais in his *On the Education of Noble Children* included one-third classical quotations out of over nine hundred ones. However, the medieval educational writers were not very generous in borrowing from their classical predicessors. In keeping the line with the medieval educational theory, they had to rewrite much of the ancient legacy. But the humanistic educators borrowed from the ancient authors more generously because they were interested mainly in the education of laymen.[4]

Thus, the chief influence of classicism on the Renaissance education was that it was meant for laymen. Its other important characteristic was that the emphasis was not so much on what was to be taught, as towards who would be taught and why.

There were some other specific issues which the humanistic educators had to face. One issue had to do with the control of education. Who should control the education? Should it be controlled by the Church or by the State? The ancient educational system was controlled either by individuals or by the State. The Athenians favoured the individualistic approach, while the Romans liked the State to control their education. The medievals preferred the Church to deal with their education. But during the Renaissance movement, the humanistic theorists supported the idea that laymen, who had genuine skills for teaching, should replace clergymen as teachers and control the education too. They did not want their institutions to be controlled by the Church.

The other important issue, which the humanistic educators considered important, was that value ought to be attached to the classics. They thought that classics had greater value than had been recognised in the Scholastic past. They considered classics better in content to any other literature which could be used in school. They saw in the classics not only literary and intellectual inspiration, but moral inspiration as well. They advised students to study Plato, Aristotle, Plutarch and many other ancient authors so that they could seek the best ways of forming character.[5]

There were some other issues relating to education, which the humanists considered of great value. For example, they thought about the problem of aim. Should education aim at knowledge or at style? They tried to pay attention to the other problems also, namely: 'Is the end of education discipline or utility?' Besides, the humanists gave more attention to the education of women. The medievals had devoted little effort to that.

In theory, physical development was of great importance but the humanists left the physical education to the school-boys' periods of free play. Music was taken to be an appropriate skill for women and was considered to lead them to appreciate life's finer things.

The humanists had quite different notions about the use of the vernacular. They considered it a vulgar tongue. They thought that a distinction was needed between a language to be used for cultural growth and one to be used for everyday speech. The language for culture was Latin, which, by then, had been clearly established as the language for learning. The various vernacular languages were used for communication and common speech only. It was not the medieval Latin which was considered to be of great value but the classical Latin which became the model in literary teaching during the Renaissance. The use of vernacular in the schools was never considered important until the fifteenth century, when the struggle between the vernacular and Latin seemed to be apparent in the field of education. Gradually, the vernacular turned the tables on Latin and became the popular medium for communication and instruction. The chief reasons for the acceptance of the vernacular were the growing nationalism and demand for a national language and a need for a national literature as well.[6]

The humanists had a better sense of history than the medieval educators. They insisted that history should occupy an important and even a central place in the school's programme, as it not only glorified the ancient civilization but was capable of upholding the patriotic sentiments. Besides, the great national Roman heroes, figured in the Roman history, were all real figures. Therefore, the humanists wanted to retain all that sort of Roman classical history as it contained the story of human bravery and moral values, which were dearer to them. The humanists themselves were realists in nature and outlook, so they acknowledged the pagan classics which had little authenticity in the Scholastic world.

The Renaissance theory of education had its weak points too. In the organisation of schools, in building a systematic curriculum, in psychological and methodological approaches to teaching, the humanists were very weak. Besides, they failed to see that order and discipline in the schools were essential to reach excellence..Most of the theories, which they thought necessary in education, could not be put into practice in the schools by the humanists.[7]

Evolution of Humanistic Education

The effects of the Renaissance movement or humanism were felt deeply in the field of education. Let us make a brief survey of the growth of humanistic education in Europe.

From the thirteenth to the fourteenth centuries, Italy witnessed a great revival of learning. Being aware of the stories of their past, the Italians developed a great interest in their classics. The two important names in the history of literature and thought in Italy during the great revival of learning are those of **Dante Alighieri** (1264-1321) and **Francesco Petrarch** (1304-1374).[8]

Dante contributed a lot to the humanistic movement. He was one of the first few early Italians, who gained a great reputation in literature. He was recognised as one of the most learned men of his days as he had a great facility in the vernacular as well as in the classical languages. Dante's *Divine Comedy*, which is written in Italian and which has abundance of references from the classical authors, is a great contribution to the educational awakening of his time.

Petrarch emphasized the significance of the classical language and literature as a basis for all education. He was responsible for the establishment of an education centre for humanistic or classical studies at the University of Padua, from where the humanistic movement obtained regular inspiration. Petrarch collected numerous classical manuscripts and made them available to students. Petrarch liked the classics, and by the force of his scholarship, he created a love and respect for them among his countrymen.[9]

It seems necessary to mention here that the Greek language had not been completely forgotten in Europe during the Middle Ages. During the time of the Renaissance, Greek was significantly revived on the Continent. The man, who played an important role in the revival of Greek, was **Emmanuel Chrysoloras** (1355-1415), who had come to Italy as a diplomat and accepted the chair in Greek at the University of Florence. In the real sense the revival of Greek in Italy began with him.[10]

With the beginning of the fourteenth century, the humanistic movement had gathered pace in Italy. By the middle of the century, Italian writers produced many important works which contained the humanistic educational theory. One of such works entitled *On Noble Character and Liberal Studies,* written by **Peter Paul Vergerious** (1349-1420), is recognised as the important work on humanistic educational theory. In it Vergerious maintained the importance of teaching of Latin literature and emphasized the need of learning for noble laymen.

Vergerious was quite familiar with the ancient classical authors, but his own views on education were of great value to the teachers of his days. Vergerious' work appeared about 1393. He touched on many topics in it, which, at that time, had great relevance to education. He discussed in it the training of children, manners, motivation for study, the capacity for accomplishment, rewards and punishment, success and failure and interest of the teachers in the students.

The course of study he recommended is a modified form of the seven liberal arts. The fundamental studies are history, ethics and eloquence which includes grammar, the rules of composition and the art of logical argument. Poetry is suggested as an occupation for leisure hours. He added a new note for the study of nature. He said that the knowledge of nature was most delightful and a profitable study for the youth.[11]

By the time Vergerious' fame spread, more discussions had been made in connection with the ancient educational writers. For the Renaissance educators, who were interested in dealing with the theory of education, four of the most important ancient theoretical works, the *Republic* of Plato, *Politics* of Aristotle, *the Orator* of Cicero and *Institutes of Oratory* of Quintillian, had been available. From a study of these authors and from a study of the ancient forms of education, the humanistic theorists were able to construct a theory of education which made possible a new order of schools.

Vittorino de Feltre (1378-1446) was another important humanist who was known as the foremost school master of the Renaissance. He was the man who conducted one of the important schools of the new order and contributed to the theoretical aspect of education, which was of great importance to his contemporaries.

The educators, who were Vittorino's contemporaries, are: **Leonardo Bruni D'Arezzo** (1369-1444), **A. Sylvius Piccolomini** (1405-1464), **Leone Battista Alberti** (1404-1472), **Battista Guarino** (1434-1513) and **Baldassare Castiglione** (1478-1529).[12] All these humanistic educators played important roles in the evolution of educational thought and practice during the Renaissance period. Their impact was great, yet compared with the influence of Vittorino de Feltre, it was relatively less strong.

Vittorino did not write books but some of his letters have been the subject of careful study. It was as a schoolmaster that Vittorino achieved great fame. One often reads about him that he was the most famous schoolmaster of the Renaissance. There may be hardly any extravagance in the claims that besides being a famous schoolmaster, he was also the greatest teacher of his time.

Neither the details of Vittorino's early life nor the educational course that he pursued at the University of Padua are clearly known. It is said that after taking his degree in arts he remained at or near the University of Padua for about twenty years. For a short time he became a member of the university faculty as the master of rhetoric. He could not continue in that position for more than a year because he felt that the discipline of the students was too bad.

In 1423 he was invited by the Lord of Mantua to conduct a court school for the children of the Conzaga family and for the children of the nobles of his court. Vittorino accepted the invitation and continued there until his death in 1446. Besides the Gonzaga children in Vittorino's school, other children from the vicinity were also admitted. The school was situated in a villa. It was called 'Pleasant House' by the Duke of Mantua. Vittorino tried to provide the school with the sort of background which brought pleasure only. He always wanted his school to be bright and cheerful. The children, who attended the school, lived there. It was a kind of home for them and Vittorino was responsible for their moral formation and their physical welfare.

History of ethics was one of the important subjects in the school. Besides the seven liberal arts, Latin was taught at the school. Greek was also taught but it was never taught on a very advanced level. The use of the vernacular was limited and was used when the children were at play.

The techniques of instruction, employed at the school, consisted partly of dictation of texts, notes, and translations and partly of oral questioning. Recitation was also practised. Reading aloud was a regular feature of the school. Since there were a number of teachers who assisted Vittorino in the school, good personal contact with each student, was made by the teachers. Being a humanist Vittorino's approach towards learning is fresh and attractive. In his school, he insisted upon the importance of variety in all the periods set aside for instruction. In actual methods of instruction, we find a definite contrast between those of Vittorino and those of the medieval schools. His school was bright and cheerful and his relations with the children were excellent. He had a great genius for teaching and his humanistic approach and outlook brought him great fame.[13]

Further Growth of Humanism

The spirit of humanism in the south of Europe was obsessed with the individual objectives but in the north its trends were quite different. There were social rather than the individual objectives which dominated the humanistic outlook in the north. The humanist educators who belong to northern Europe are: Guillaume Bude, Peter Ramus, Colet, Elyot, More, Erasmus and Vives. Bude and Ramus belonged to France; Colt, Elyot and More hailed from England; Erasmus was Dutch and Vives belonged to Spain. Of all these northern humanists the important figures, from the point of view of history of education, were Vives and Erasmus.[14] Let us examine their thought and impact on education during the Renaissance.

Desiderius Erasmus (1469-1536)

Erasmus was a complex, versatile and talented man. As a monk, Erasmus found life in the monastry so oppressive that he spent very little time there. He left the monastry whenever he could and very often did not try to seek the permission of his superiors for his travels.[15]

Erasmus attended the schools of Brethren of the Common Life, the university of Paris and for a brief time, Cambridge. Gradually he became the greatest scholar of his age.

As a good humanist, Erasmus hoped to refine taste, purify morals, eradicate ecclesiastical abuses, and promote unity, peace and harmony in European Society. He believed he had a mission, which was to lay the groundwork for learning and living which should be productive of wisdom. He assumed: The classics contain a wisdom worth having and men must find the proper means for assimilating it.[16]

Erasmus was greatly inspired by the classical educators. He even longed to excel and improve upon the methods of teaching provided by the classical theorists. He considered Latin and Greek to be means to an end and encouraged the study of both language and literature as the means to character formation.

Erasmus' influence in the educational arena remained for four hundred years. His impact on education can be classified as under:

(i) He wrote two famous books, *The Right Methods of Instruction* and *The Liberal Education for Boys,* wherein he showed clearly the importance of the use of the techniques of imitation.

(ii) He prepared models and textbooks which could be used by teachers and students to understand the classical literature better.

(iii) He developed a theory of humanistic education which was based on the classical knowledge, which would lead students to develop a better moral character.

Erasmus' two principal works, *The Right Method of Instruction* and *The Liberal Education of Boys,* provide great guidance for the educators. The first book contains 'what sort of right methods are to be used in teaching the classics and understanding the classical authors!' Erasmus is one of the few educationists who attached greater importance to the methods of instructions which included the choice of material as well as the means employed in providing knowledge. He insisted that the right methods of instruction would always help in a better understanding of Latin and Greek and promote scholarship in boys. He emphasised that one should devote more attention to the child's early years in learning. In this respect he followed Quintillian, who would never allow any sort of wrong learning at the earlier stages of the childs development. Erasmus' *The Right Method of Instruction* is a great educational document of fine quality. It influenced educators not only during the Renaissance period but for many centuries after him.

The Liberal Education of Boys is Erasmus' most mature book which deals with the aim of education. He thought that educational objectives ought to lead men towards knowledge, honesty and independent judgment. He believed that sound education was the essential condition to reach real wisdom. Since the aim of education is to produce man of character, he thought that classical literature should dominate the curriculum, for its study could lead men to conceive moral ideals.

Besides Quintilian's influence, Plato's impact can be traced on him too. For example, a similarity can be seen between Erasmus' views expressed on man's need for education and Plato's ideas on the same subject. Erasmus reflected:[17]

> "It is beyond dispute that man not instructed through reason in philosophy and sound learning is a creature lower than a brute, seeing that there is no beast more wild or more harmful than a man who is driven hither and thither by ambition or desire, anger or envy, or lawless temper".

Thus, Erasmus recognises the importance of reason. He insists that growth of reason is very essential for it enables man to unite in a community and helps him to perpetuate his culture.

On the issue of individual progress Erasmus said that three conditions could determine the child's progress in school. They are nature, training and practice. By nature he meant innate capacity for achievement and a natural motivation to reach excellence. By training he meant the instruction and guidance that the student could be able to obtain. By practice he intended a free exercise by the student of that capacity which nature had implanted in him.[18] He added: "Nature without skill training must be imperfect, and practice without the method, which training supplies, leads to hopeless confusion".[19]

Erasmus' principal ideas, contained in his chief educational works, can be summarized in the following way:[20]

(i) He recognised the worth of physical education but he did not give much attention to it in any school programme.
(ii) He acknowledged the rights of the middle class people for educational opportunity. He was unwilling to provide education to 'a class'.
(iii) He recognised the individual differences and special talents among children but he proposed the well-sounded, generally educated and culturally competent individual.
(iv) His own observations led him to reflect that a child should begin formal schooling at the age of seven.
(v) He preferred a classical oriented curriculum in which language was emphasised as a tool to gain good experience.
(vi) He was an open-minded person as he wanted the school's door to remain open for all subjects. The curriculum was open to all necessary areas of experience and the school-room was a forum in which all questions could be discussed.
(vii) He proposed a theory of education aimed at the classics. He thought that the study of classics was very essential to achieve the highest goal of humanistic education, which was moral virtue.

Juan Luis Vives (1492-1540)

Vives was born in Spain. He began his career as a Scholastic educator and later on converted to humanism under the ardent influence of Erasmus.

Vives was more practical in his outlook than his predecessor. He put humanistic education to the realistic practices by providing the school's curriculum instructions in a more practical manner. It helped student to develop skill in daily living. He justified useful knowledge and thought of schooling as the period, which would provide students with the opportunity to learn something well and useful in life. Thus, he was more of a realist than any of his contemporaries.[21]

Beginning with Vives and looking into his interests in the pedagogical practices, a decline in humanistic trends is witnessed. So he stands at the end of an era which had been strongly influenced by Erasmus and at the beginning of a new one which is marked with the beginning of the science of pedagogy.[22]

Vives's important works reflect his deep interest in educational psychology. *His On Poor Relief* contains his interest in the plight of the poor and of social problems prevalent at that time. His *De Anima* or *Concerning the Soul* reflects the relationship between learning and psychology. Because of his work, *On the Instruction of Christian Women* and because of his appointment as a tutor to the Princess Mary of England, Vives has often been considered a pioneer who tried to provide opportunities for the education of women. The following are Vives' important views on his educational theory:[23]

(i) Vives recognised that the basic foundation of education was laid down in the home during the early years of the child. So he emphasised the importance of the role of parents in the education of their children.

(ii) He said that children should be sent to school at the age of seven.

(iii) Vives reflected that public schools were better than the private schools. So he preferred, like the other humanists, that boys should be educated in public schools as they would enjoy greater opportunities for learning within a group.

(iv) Vives regarded education as a public responsibility and thought that the public ought to pay for it.

(v) As a humanist, he supported the idea that the environment in which teaching and learning take place should be pleasant and conducive to learning. He recommended the inclusion of sports, drama and other sorts of recreation in the educational programme.

(vi) He did not approve a complete imitation of the classics but he stressed that one should accept the values reflected in the classics. He advised teaching in the vernacular in the schools and insisted that it should be used as a means to introduce Latin to students.

(vii) Vives was considered to be the chief mover for greater opportunities for the education of women. He suggested for them a careful study of the vernacular, Latin, religion and moral precepts. He wanted them to develop good conduct and to keep care of children and household management.

(viii) Vives emphasised the importance of learning history and the natural sciences in school.

REFERENCES

1. Bolgar, R.R. (1954), *The Classical Heritage and Its Beneficiaries*, (New York: Cambridge University Press), pp. 260-268.
2. Power, *History of Education*, pp. 336-340.
3. Power, *History of Education*, pp. 336-337.
4. Daniel D. MeGarry (1954), "Renaissance Educational Theory", *Historical Bulletin*, Vol. 32, pp. 195-209.
5. Mason, J.E. (1935), *Gentlefolk in the Making*, (Philadelphia; University of Pennsylvania Press), pp. 40-71.
6. Power, *History of Education*, pp. 340-42.
7. Power, *History of Education*, pp. 343.
8. Baron Hans (1966), *The Crisis of the Early Italian Renaissance*; (Princeton: Princeton University Press), pp. 200-210.
9. Wilkins, Ernest H. (1961), *Life of Petrarch*; (Chicago: University of Chicago Press); and Power, *op.cit.*, pp. 344-45.
10. Bolgar, *The Classical Heritage and its Beneficiaries*, pp. 265-71.
11. Boyd, *History of Western Education*, pp. 163-64.
12. Woodward Willian H. (1924), *Studies in Education During the Age of the Renaissance, 1400-1600*, pp. 45-65. (New York: Cambridge University Press).
13. Power, *History of Education*, pp. 356-59.
14. Power, *History of Education*, p. 360.
15. Hyma Albert (1930), *Erasmus and the Humanists*, (New York: F.S. Crofts & Co.) pp. 45-51.
16. Woodwards William H. (1904), *Desiderius Erasmus, Concerning the Aim and Method of Education*, (New York: Cambridge University Press), pp. 163-64.
17. Woodwards, *Erasmus*, p. 186.
18. Power, *History of Education*, p. 372.
19. Woodwards, *Erasmus*, p. 191.
20. Power, *History of Education*, pp. 374-76.
21. Power, *History of Education*, pp. 377.
22. Weiss Robert (1957), *Humanism in England During the Fifteenth Century*, (Oxford: B. Blackwell), pp. 96-99.
23. Power, *History of Education*, pp. 378-79.

CHAPTER-VI

REVOLT AGAINST CATHOLIC TRADITIONS

Fifteenth century Europe was a scene of new inventions. By the opening of new scientific and geographic worlds, the European society began to wear a new face. It was the time when the humanistic movement was at its peak. In Italy and in southern Europe, humanism was aristocratic and individualistic but in northern Europe, the movement became more religious, moral and social. Education in the north of Europe, specially in the hands of Erasmus and Vives, became a means for social and moral reforms.

In the north as well as the south of Europe the humanistic scholars were opposed to scholastic philosophy and its authoritarian attitude. In the north of Europe the opposition took the form of protests against the doctrines of the Catholic Church, and resulted in the demands for a return to simple and non-ritualistic devotions.[1]

The conditions of study and thought had already been revolutionized due to increase in the number of universities. The new inventions, specially that of the printing machine, made learning easier and more widely available. It helped the common men understand the humanistic trends more vividly. The growing opposition between scholastics and humanists gradually resulted in refashioning the trends of the Church in accordance with the naturalistic standards of classical virtue, which had upheld the importance of natural goodness of man in the past.

Besides, a general laxity within the Catholic Church, together with the other conditions present in the society at that time, also resulted in the revolt against the Church. The authority of the Pope had been slackened and most of the clergy had started leaning towards a spirit of worldliness. The later fifteenth century witnessed the popes to be more interested in consolidating their political powers and maintaining their financial position, rather than concentrating on religious matters. It resulted in a deep discontent against the authority of the papal popes and a demand for reforms in the Church. The prominent educationists, whose names are linked with the religious revolt during the fifteenth century, are Martin Luther, Philip Melanchthon and John Sturn.

Martin Luther (1483-1546)

In his fear for the future of human learning, Erasmus left out of his reckoning the constructive genius of Luther. Luther did not, perhaps, attach the same importance to the study of the classics as Erasmus, but the point of view of the great religious pioneer was not so different from that of the great scholar. In their common revolt against the medieval system of life, both went to the past for their ideas of social regeneration.[2]

Martin Luther was a son of a lower middle-class miner. He was born in Eisleben. Luther started his early schooling at Mansfield and later on he went to Magdeburg to study under the Brethren of the Common Life. Not much more than that is known of his life or schooling on the pre-university levels.[3]

At the age of eighteen, Luther started his university studies at Erfurt, which was then considered Germany's one of the finest universities. At Erfurt, he pursued the studies of liberal arts and philosophy and came in contact with the masters of great reputations. In 1505, when he was about to take his master's degree in arts, he began the study of law. But soon he abandoned his studies and turned to the monastic life. He entered the Augustinian monastery at Erfurt on July 17, 1505.[4]

A few months after he entered the monastery he was ordained a priest. Then he undertook formal technological studies and completed them in about eighteen months. From 1508 to 1511 he worked as a lecturer of ethics and theology in Wittenberg and Erfurt respectively, and performed other ecclesiastical duties. In 1512 he obtained his degree as doctor of theology. In 1513 he was appointed professor of theology at the university of Wittenberg.

His duties at the university and the demand for his time in his office of superior of the religious community kept him busy for many years. Sometimes when he had to go out into the affairs of the world, he felt that he was not able to fulfil all the religious obligations prescribed by the Church. It was the beginning of his dissatisfaction towards his religious vocation. Gradually, great frustration rose within him and he started ignoring the rules of monastic life. He then began to choose and rely on his own strength built on faith. Finally, on October 31, 1517, he presented his ninety-five theses to the Church at Wittenberg and openly participated in the great Revolt against the ecclesiastical practices.[5]

Although Luther was a religious reformer, we find him framing an educational theory in sermons and religious tracts. He was keenly interested to educational theory in general, and to humanistic promises and practices in particular. Luther, in fact, constructed only a framework for education, and left it for others to work out the details.[6]

One of his first statements on education, which is also considered to be the first Protestant revolt-document on education, was *A Letter to the Mayors and Aldermen of All Cities of Germany on Behalf of Christian Schools.* Luther addressed this letter to the officials concerned with the schools' administration. The letter reminded them to build schools and to replace those which had been destroyed due to the Protestant Revolt.[7] The letter contained a strong conviction that spiritual benefits could be drawn from the right kind of education, which could be achieved through the study and understanding of the scriptures.

The theory of education propounded by Luther, was based on his love of God and his devotion to his country—Germany. To obtain both, required the presence of educated men only. The study of the Bible was then imperative. So like the humanists, who had advocated the study of ancient languages, Luther looked with favour on the study of languages.

Luther found humanistic education appealing, His *Sermon on the Duty of Sending Children to School,* which he delivered in 1530, contains his strong educational views. In the *Sermon* he showed a great concern for the education of children and for the dignity of the teacher. He reflected:

> 'Where were your supply of preachers, jurists and physicians, if the art of grammar and rhetoric had no existence? These are the foundation, out of which they all flow. I tell you in a word that a diligent, devoted school teacher, preceptor or any person, no matter what his title, who faithfully trains and teaches boys, can never receive adequate reward, and no money is sufficient to pay the debt you own him'.[8]

Luther divided the *Sermon* into two parts. The first part dealt with the moral and spiritual gains which the children would get by attending school. The second part described the worldly benefits. In the first part Luther appealed to the parents under his own religious jurisdiction to send their bright boys to school to prepare for the Christian Ministry. It was at this point that he emphasised the need to study the classical languages so that the study of scripture could be promoted. In the second part he addressed the well-educated boys and young men to do their duty to the state.

On the subject of method, he seemed to have perceived in advance that the realistic ideology was going to pervade the educational arena, so he suggested that the natural activity of the child should be utilized in learning. He opposed any method which would repress a child's nature. He advocated the use of concrete examples in teaching and condemned grammatical approach to the teaching of languages for he thought that it was somewhat unnatural.

Luther, in fact, wanted a system of education as free and unrestricted as the Gospel he preached: indifferent, like the Gospel to distinctions of sex or of social class. He did not ignore the difficulties that universal education presented on the economic side. He knew that many of the parents were very poor, and that the time required for the education of their children could sometimes be ill spared. He met the difficulty by suggesting that both boys and girls should be sent to school for an hour or two a day and should at the same time be learning some handicraft at home. He had a scheme for a broad type of education, under which he sketched out that children should learn not only the languages and history, but singing and music and the different branches of mathematics as well.[9]

Philip Melanchthon (1497-1560)

The force which provided movement to Lutheran educational concepts, was Philip Melanchthon. Luther looked at education through the eyes of a preacher but Melanchthon was an educator who was more anxious to act as Luther's educational lieutenant.[10] Both Luther and Melanchthon supported the theory that the Bible and the Catechism should have an important place in the school syllabus.

Philip Melanchthon's early career started with scholastic type of education. First he studied logic, scholastic philosophy and then took his master's degree in arts at Tubingen and began lecturing on grammar and rhetoric.[11] It was during the time he was teaching that he became a full advocate of humanism. He rejected the scholastic practice of teaching grammar as a branch of logic and favoured the study of the classical authors.

It was when Melanchthon was working as the professor of Greek at the University of Wittenberg that he was offered the professorship in theology as well. Now Melanchthon had a great opportunity to test the assumptions that classical studies were useful to theology. His academic experience proved that his assumptions were true. Since then he became a Christian humanist. He began to think that the purpose of education was to provide the student with a comprehensive meaning of the world. To achieve this great purpose, the curriculum must concentrate on language study, which makes an essential contribution to understanding.

Melanchthon was a practical person. He reflected that 'the goal of classical study was to produce a confirmed Christian who could write, speak and think clearly about the important questions of the day'.[12] Thus, he brought humanism down to a level, which, when applied to educational practices, was thought to be useful to educate the entire Christian community.

Melanchthon's Christian humanism consists of three educational positions: (a) it has a medieval outlook as it stresses to achieve a comprehensive meaning of the world; (b) it emphasizes the study of the classical languages to broaden the understanding; (c) it consists of the idea of unchanging human love for God. Most of his ideas were embraced by the educators of his own time and by those who came after him. One of the important schoolmen and a distinguished Protestant, who was greatly influenced by him, was John Sturm.

John Sturm (1507-1589)

John Sturm's elementary education was completed in the Court School. After his elementary schooling, he spent three years with the famous Brethren of the Common Life. Then he spent five years at the university of Louvain. After completing his formal education at Louvain, he spent a short time in the university of Paris. Then he was invited by the town fathers to become rector of the Gymnasium at Strassburg where he remained at the position for forty-five years.

When Sturm reached Stressburg and assumed as rector, he found the town operating three Latin schools, which were functioning according to Melanchthon's humanistic plans. But the schools were not functioning as effectively as Sturm had thought. Therefore, first of all, he consolidated them into one school. Then he framed a plan to run that school. That plan was laid down by him in his book entitled *The Best Mode of Opening an Institution of Learning*. The book was a sort of guide for his teachers to run the school effectively. It touched every phase of the school's operation. As long as Sturm remained at the school, his plan which he contained in the book to operate the school, hardly altered. Perhaps the main change from the original plan was the substitution of a nine-year programme for the ten-year course which had been originally proposed.

The Gymnasium, with a nine-year school programme, became the supreme model for all modern secondary education. Sturm had three goals to operate the classical Gymnasium; piety, knowledge and the art of speaking.

In order to develop piety in the pupils, religious instructions were carefully planned and the classes were supervised. To achieve knowledge and eloquences, Sturm built the school curriculum around Latin. The curriculum Sturm organised, aimed directly at achieving the superior goal of oral and written eloquence. He did not allow the teaching of the vernacular. Neither geography, history, science, nor mathematics was taught. Greek and Latin language and literature formed the core of all studies. The scriptures were read in Greek and Latin and the teaching of logic involved a thorough knowledge of Latin.

Each class had its authors (Homer, Virgil, Cicero and St. Paul) and the achievement at the lower grades were taken to be the foundation for the next higher grade. Thus, the students were promoted from one grade to another when they had achieved sufficiently well at the previous grade.[13]

Sturm's school plan was extra-ordinary and it brought him success and fame. All over Europe and in America as well, his brand of secondary schools was accepted and adopted. In fact, his school programme, though narrowed down, contained the content which was confirmed by learning's best traditions [14]

Other Protestant Educators

Besides Luther, Melanchthon and Sturm, there were such men as John Bugenhagen, John Brenz, Ulrich Zwingli, John Calvin and Mathurin Cordier, who accepted the basic religious doctrines of the Revolt and felt the need for revising the existing system of education.

Bugenhagen (1485-1558) achieved a good reputation as an organiser of schools in northern Germany. Besides the Latin schools, which formed a part of the system he had created, he became interested in the schools in German for certain children of the lower and middle classes. He went ahead with his plans and succeeded to some extent. It was as a result of his work that the vernacular schools became popular.[15]

Though **Zwingli** (1484-1534) and **Calvin** (1509-1564) are not considered to be the great champions of educational reforms, Calvinistic religious reflections had a great impact on educational attitudes. Calvin greatly influenced the direction and purpose of education. Both in Europe and America, Calvinism made inroads, its doctrines representing a world view. Zwingli was a religious reformer who severed all connections with the Catholic Church. He insisted on bringing improvement to schools in the sense that he wanted them to become timely established. He saw that they were closely supervised and that they held to their original aim, that is. to teach the knowledge of God.

Cordier's (1479-1564) pedagogy was based on the assumption that fluency in Latin should be taken as an achievement of decent education. With this assumption he formulated a school curriculum which aimed directly at linguistic skills.

Cordier's practical influences on school's curricula was great. He can be seen as the real representative of a kind of humanism which won a place for itself in western secondary education. His views on education were greatly accepted by most of the religiously minded teachers of the sixteenth and seventeenth centuries.[16]

Broad Influence of Protestanism on Schools

As a result of the Protestant Revolt, schools started changing their faces in Europe. The municipal schools, which had been regularly organised in Europe since medieval times, conceded greatly to Protestant influences. They abandoned most of the scholastic courses and set a course of their own, admitting the vernacular as a subject of study. They also started allowing girls to study in the same class-rooms as boys. The spirit of Protestantism was taken as a charter of independence for town schools. Many of the municipal schools became free schools. Though this independence seldom affected the quality of learning, it put the schools in a more favourable position as they now received more funds from the town treasury and the public as well.[17]

In England, the Revolt was led by King Henry VIII. It resulted in the abolition of the monastic institutions and to the confiscation of their property. The court schools or the palace schools, which dated back from the time of Charles the Great, were closed because of Henry's religious revolt. Thus, Henry attempted a complete break with the past. The instructions were now given in English and the tools of such instruction were the Catechism. Primers were also written in English. This move provided the vernacular a principal position as a language of instruction. It was quite a significant change which came to the schools in England and Ireland as well.[18]

The new schools, especially the favoured colleges of Oxford and Cambridge, received most of the funds which had been confiscated from the religious houses. From this time onwards, royal patronage to education became a precedent. But the schools and colleges gradually lost their independence as they became more dependent on the state treasury. However, the newly emerged schools had some of the following new features:[19]

(1) They prescribed the universal education for the rich and the poor alike.
(2) They followed the idea of a unified system of national schools by which the pupils with the requisite ability might attain the highest positions. The Genevan academy, like the medieval universities, was at once an elementary school, a secondary school and a university. In the Scottish scheme, the different grades of learning were definitely separated and yet all contributed to the final result.
(3) A clear scheme of education for different stages came into existence through these schools. The pupil would spend two years in learning reading, Catechism and the elements of grammar, then pass to a town grammar school to study grammar and Latin for three to four years. Next, he would go for four years to a higher school or college to study logic, rhetoric and the ancient languages (including Greek). Finally, he would go to the university for three years to study a course of philosophy which was followed by a course in law, medicine or theology, which he would complete about his twenty-fifth year.

The Jesuit System of Education

As a result of the Protestant Revolt, a renewal of interest in education and the management of schools grew in the Roman Catholic Churches. It gave birth to two new religious groups, the Jesuits and the Ursulines. These two new groups laboured in the field of Catholic education and achieved a reputation for effective teaching in the educational world.

The first teaching order of women, the Ursulines establishment in the Church, were founded by St. Angela Merici in 1535. St. Angela, with the help of twelve companions, founded the Ursulines. This community of religious women since then have done important educational work down through the years.[20]

Among many religious communities of men, the society of Jesus has gained greater fame. Many religious orders within the Catholic Church did outstanding work for the developments of Catholic education, but for all the excellence that may be claimed for the Brethren of the Common Life, the Jesuits occupy a great position. The Jesuits challenged the Protestant schools in their own lands and established a system which gathered great popularity.

The pioneer of this movement was a Spanish nobleman, Ignatius of **Loyola** (1491-1556). He worked as a soldier up to the age of thirty but while recovering from a serious wound, he happened to read the books, Life of *Christ* and the *Lives of Saints.* He was influenced by these books then he renounced his worldly ambitions and devoted himself to a ascetic life.

In order to compensate for the loss of his early education, he went to different schools and universities for a few years until he reached Paris. In Paris he gathered round him a small company of like-minded students and with five of them formed in 1534 a new religious order called the Society of Jesus, which had for its first objectives a missionary pilgrimage to Jerusalem.[21]

The secret of the success of the Society of Jesus can be traced partly to the fine enthusiasm and devotion with which they combined learning and piety in the performance of their duties. Partly it was due to Loyola, who had a deep insight into the needs of the age. Besides, great care was given to the preparation of the members of the Society for their work as teachers and professors. The teachers had to spend their first two years in the study of philosophy in the lowest classes of the gymnasium. Sometime later they proceeded to the study of theology or other branches of higher learning, and then qualified themselves to become teachers of philosophy. Ultimately they became professors of subjects in which they specialized.

The devotion and enthusiasm implicit in the members of the Society and the good procedure of selection and training of teachers, soon brought popularity to it. Many new colleges came into being in a few years of time, but by the eighteenth century the Jesuit schools and colleges became out of touch with the spirit of the age dominated by scientific thought.[22]

REFERENCES

1. Power, *History of Education*, p. 382.
2. Boyd, *History of Western Education*, p. 187.
3. Friedenthal Richard (1967), *Luther*, (Munchen: Sein Leben and Seihe Zeit), pp. 15-30.
4. Richard, *Luther*, pp. 25-30.
5. Boehmer Heinrich (1946), *Road to Reformation*, (Philadelphia: Muhlenberg Press), pp. 73-80.
6. Power, *History of Education*, pp. 385-86.
7. In Germany before the Protestant Revolt, schools were conducted and owned by the Roman Catholic Church. Therefore, little educational opportunity was offered outside Church-related institutions. At the time of the Revolt, Church-owned assets and school buildings were confiscated by princes, nobles and State officers. Many school buildings

were destroyed and converted for different sorts of uses. In the wake of the Protestant Revolt, the bulk of education was simply in ruins.

8. Quoted by Eby Frerick (1931), *Early Protestant Educators*, (New York: McGraw Hill Book Co.), p. 144.
9. Boyd, *History of Western Education*, pp. 189-90.
10. Bolgar, *Classical Heritage*, p. 344.
11. Manschreek, C.L. (1958), *Melanchthon, the Quiet Reformer*, (New York: Abingdon Press), p. 49.
12. Power, *History of Education*, p. 391.
13. Power, *History of Education*, pp. 394-95.
14. Laurie, S.S. (1903), *Studies in the History of Educational Opinion from the Renaissance*, (New York: Cambridge University Press), Chapter III.
15. Ruccius, Walter M. (1916), *John Bugenhagen Pomeranus* (Philadelphia: The United Lutheran Publishing House), p. 75.
16. Power, *History of Education*, p. 398
17. Power, *History of Education*, pp. 398-99.
18. Power, *History of Education*, p. 399.
19. Boyd, *History of Western Education*, pp. 202-03.
20. Power, *History of Education*, p. 401.
21. Boyd, *History of Western Education*, pp. 203-05.
22. Boyd, *History of Western Education*, p. 206.

CHAPTER-VII

THE INTRODUCTION OF REALISM IN EDUCATION

Scholasticism and humanism, despite their impact on school learning, came to the brink of failure after the passage of time. The academic theories, propounded by their scholars, made great changes in the field of learning, but they could not include much of life's ardent realities in the school programme. So, a change was inevitable.

Besides, the reformed churches gradually lost their hold on the schools with the development of the secular spirit. With poorly equipped schools and badly paid teachers, the quality of education started declining. By the end of the sixteenth century a broad wave of educational stagnation swept throughout Europe.[1]

The beginning of the seventeenth century was a promising display of educational enterprise in various parts of Europe. During this century, anything which did not reflect in the school curriculum about human needs and aspiration, was rejected. It was a new approach to learning which focussed its attention on life's persistent needs. This new wave of thinking gradually swept across Europe and brought deep and far reaching effects on education. This was the beginning of the realistic movement in education. During this age of realism, through a careful observation of nature and of social institutions, knowledge could be verified empirically and was accepted. As a large amount of scientific knowledge became available, the old theories about human life became obsolete.

The principal scientific innovators of this century were Descartes, Galileo, Stevin, Newton, Gilbert and Harvey. These scientists revised the knowledge in the fields of mathematics, astronomy, instrumentation, mechanics, geography and other areas of human learning. Now, content need not to take the work of traditional authority. It was filled in with the newly discovered scientific knowledge, which had empiric foundations.[2]

The scientific achievements opened new avenues between knowledge and social progress in the world. Methods of finding dependable knowledge were tested. New and older techniques were discarded if they were found wanting. School practices were re-examined and efforts were made to bring the newly discovered scientific knowledge to the classrooms by revising curricula.[3]

Educators, social reformers and scientists tried to conceive the notion of realism from different angles. On the educational level, realistic emphasis was either psychologically or humanistically orientated. All the realistic educators emphasized that learning must have real data and what was taught in the school's curriculum must be valid and meaningful, and be capable of practical application. The humanistic realists, on the other hand, believed that proper use of language was of great utility. They thought that though science was the key to producing dependable knowledge, language was still the means of communicating it. **John Milton** (1608-1674), a humanistic realist, besides appreciating the progress of the scientists, insisted on a school programme which had language and literature as important items of its curriculum.[4]

The social realists were eager to bring social reforms by coming directly into contact with society's institutions. They advised their students to use society itself as their school.[5]

John Amos Comenius, one of the leading realists of the age, emphasized that knowledge of psychology was of great importance. He pointed out that schools' curriculum must consist of all worth-while knowledge—scientific, literary and social, and the bases of learning should not only be psychological but also physiological. He seemed to be greatly interested in imparting the fundamentals of universal wisdom to his pupils by using a method which began on the sensory level.[6]

Thus, the seventeenth century realism was many-sided and its chief exponents were John Amos Comenius and John Locke. However, the names of Francis Bacon and Rene Descartes also need to be included with them.

John Amos Comenius (1592-1670)

Comenius was born at Nivnitz in Moravia. His interest in education was awakened by the badness of his own. After four years at a village school, he went at the advanced age of fifteen to study Latin at the grammar school at Prerau. It was here that a noble man helped him to continue his studies urging him to follow priesthood.[7]

From 1612 to 1628 Comenius's life was marked by vicissitude. In

1616 he accepted a position at a school in Prague and taught there for two years. In 1618 he was made pastor of a parish in Fulnek. It was the period of the Thirty Years' War and Fulnek was a troubled area. Comenius had to go into hiding for eight years, but in 1628 he gave up the life of concealment and managed to reach Leszno in Poland, where he stayed until 1656.

Comenius's Chief Works

Throughout his life Comenius wrote many books. In 1612 he started the project of a *Czech-Latin Dictionary,* which he completed in forty years. That very year he wrote *Labyrinth of the World* in which he criticised the teaching of the seven liberal arts. In 1614 he wrote *A Theater of All Things,* which is a sixteen-volume encyclopedia in Czech. From 1628 to 1631 he wrote *Janua Linguarum Reserata.* It made him famous throughout Europe. His another important book the *Great Didactic,* which he started in 1628, was finished in 1632. Initially, this book was written in Czech but then it was translated into Latin(1657). Now his ideas on education were known far and wide.

His Views on Education

The Great Didactic is his greatest treatise on education. In it he affirms that all men could be taught all things and be made learned, virtuous and pious, provided the proper ways of instructions are followed. He writes:[8]

> "Didactic signifies the art of teaching... We venture to promise A Great Didactic, that is to say, the whole art of teaching all things to all men, and indeed of teaching them with certainty, so that the result cannot fail to follow; further, of teaching them pleasantly, that is to say, without annoyance or aversion on the part of the teacher or pupil, but rather with the greatest enjoyment for both; further of teaching them thoroughly, not superficially and slowly, but in such a manner as to lead to true knowledge to gentle morals and so the deepest piety..."

Although *The Great Didactic* belongs to the earlier period of Comenius's life, it contains his maturer thoughts about the art of teaching and the kinds of educational methods which were urgently needed to provide adequate knowledge to the students. About the deplorable conditions existent in the schools of his time Comenius wrote:[9]

"They are the terror of boys and the slaughter houses of minds—places where a hatred of literature and books is contracted, where ten or more years are spent in learning what might be acquired in one, where what ought to be poured in gently is violently forced in and beaten in, where what ought to be put clearly and perspicaciously is presented in a confused and intricate way, as if it were a collection of puzzles—places where minds are fed on words."

In line with the ideal of universal school expressed in *The Great Didactic,* Comenius would have liked to establish a system of education where all the young, whether of the rich or the poor parents, boys and girls, both noble and ignoble, in all cities and towns, villages and hamlets, should be sent to school. Comenius wanted to include girls with the boys to provide a similar kind of education. He thought that the girls possessed equal sharpness of mind and capacity for knowledge and they were able to attain the highest positions which boys could obtain.[10]

School Organisation

In *The Great Didactic* Comenius unfolds a plan how to organise schools. He conceived that there should be a nursery school for children up to the age of six. Next to the nursery school, there should be a vernacular or primary school in every village for pupils of six to twelve. After primary school a Latin school or secondary school should be available in every city for pupils of twelve to eighteen.

The secondary school should be followed by a university which would be established in every province for youths from eighteen to twenty-four preparing for his profession.[11]

Theory of Education

Comenius's views about the methods of instruction, curriculum, school discipline, individual differences, size of the class and stages of schooling are worth mentioning. His views are summarised as under:[12]

Methods of Instruction

Comenius was deeply distressed because of the teachers' lack of knowledge of teaching methods. He felt that each teacher used a different method which did not bring any good results.

To remedy the defect he proposed that there should be only one teacher in each class, and only one author should be used for each subject studied. Everything should be taught thoroughly, briefly and pithily. Things which are naturally connected need to be taught in combination. Subjects should be taught in graded steps and the work of the one day should be expanded out of the previous days' work. The things which are of no value, must be discarded.

The instructions should not only be methodical but also be agreeable to the pupils. Comenius was of the opinion that the child should be first instructed in things before he is expected to express them in language. As far as possible he must learn to know and observe the things himself.

Talking on certain maximum of teaching method Comenius proclaimed that the teacher should proceed from easy to difficult and all things which are naturally connected ought to be taught in combination. He said that nothing should be taught the young ones unless it is demanded by their age and mental capacity.

Comenius believed that if the principle of order is followed in the school, all the errors of the past can be avoided. Accordingly, he contended that the art of teaching demands the skilful arrangement of time, of the subjects taught and of the method.

School Subject

Comenius would like to include in the school curriculum all those subjects which can make a man wise, virtuous and pious. It is not necessary that all knowledge of sciences and arts is to be imparted but the principles, the causes, the uses of all the most important things in existence, are to be taught. He also advocated the necessity of the use of the mother tongue, specially at the primary school level.

School Discipline

On school discipline Comenius had views similar to Quintilian. He remarked that no punishment should be given for lack of readiness to learn. The teacher needs to employ sympathetic treatment to invoke love of learning into the minds of pupils. Any other procedure would only bring antipathy and dislike towards learning.

Individual Differences

Considering that children differ in their capacities and that education need not be identical for all, Comenius condemned the condition prevalent in the seventeenth century schools. He advocated that schools must be made available to all and teachers must adopt an approach that would make learning more pleasant. Since he acknowledged the differences in the intellectual capacities of children, he suggested that the brighter students should assist in the instruction of slower ones. The instruction must recognise individual differences.[13]

Size of Classes

Comenius believed that large classes were necessary at that time from a social point of view, and that they were also desirable educationally. He thought that the teachers would be more attentive to their work if their classes were large. By large classes he meant possibly as many as two hundred students, but he advised to have systematic sectioning of students, with key students supervising and tutoring, perhaps twenty others.[14]

Different Stages of Learning

Comenius recognised seven stages of learning.[15] The seven stages or schools are: (1) the antenatal (2) infancy (3) boyhood (4) adolescence (5) youth (6) adulthood, and (7) senescence; death completes the series.

The first school has its location in the womb, the second in every home, the third in every village, the fourth in every town, the fifth in every kingdom or province, the sixth in the whole world and the seventh wherever old men congregate.

Thus, all life is to be a school from the cradle, or even prior, to the grave. Provisions for each stage of life in the way of schools, books and teachers must be made. The aim should be to bring to a successful conclusion what had already been begun. All the stages of learning, therefore, are of great importance.

Comenius throughout his writings reflected a sincere sympathy with childhood. He wanted education to be available to all. He wanted the children to learn in an environment of happiness created by a human treatment. It has been claimed that the establishment of the United Nations Educational, Scientific and Cultural Organisation (UNESCO) marks the culmination of a movement for the creation of an international agency for education which began with Comenius.[16]

Francis Bacon (1561-1626)

In the history of education Francis Bacon will be remembered mainly as he reflected strongly that induction could be a means of obtaining knowledge. Then with the same zeal he stressed that knowledge should be used.[17] No one more than Bacon popularized the idea of equating knowledge and power, says Edward J. Power. Bacon reflected: "Human knowledge and human power meet in one". Thus, Bacon's reflections exerted a strong influence on the realistic movement during the seventeenth century.

Becon's principal writings are *Novum Organum, New Atlantis* and the *Advancement of Learning.*

In *Novum Organum* Bacon idealised induction as a way of gathering more knowledge and to draw new meaning out of the things already known.

In *New Atlantis* he shows us how men can lead ideal lives if they follow certain social, political and intellectual ways. He further reflects in it how to make use of inductive techniques and the newly discovered knowledge.

Like the other realists of his age, he stressed upon man's need for knowing the real, physical world in which he lived. He also emphasized the need to convert knowledge to useful social purposes.

Rene Descartes (1596-1650)

Like Bacon, Descartes was also not interested in pedagogical issues. On philosophical plain, he reflected a unique combination of idealism and realism. His "Cogito ergo sum" (I think, therefore, I exist) and his 'Ontological argument' for the existence of God... "I am able to think of God, a perfect being, because God has implanted the idea"... placed him on common ground with orthodox idealists.[18]

Thus, Descartes's main concern was philosophy, but his system of thought certainly affected education. He was impressed with mathematics as a principal means for obtaining positive knowledge about the mechanism of nature, and he was no less impressed with the power of human minds to construct a mathematical apparatus and use it to achieve certitude. In this way he brought a new wave to the realm of education. The precision and certitude made evident in mathematics were transferred to all human problems, and realist educators could easily see great educational promise in their emancipation from the humanistic and scholastics theories of the past.[19]

John Locke (1632-1704)

Locke was born in Wrington, England. He received a good education at Westminster School and at Christ Church College, Oxford. He entered Oxford at the age of twenty and was still there when he was fifty, as he was working on a studentship at that time. During his long academic career he studied Greek, rhetoric and ethics. He taught many subjects and tutored hundreds of students. Finally, he finished his university course with a medical degree.[20]

His written works disclose his versatile genius which could include easily the fields of government, philosophy, economics, education and religion with equal intensity and depth.

Locke's Educational Theory

Locke stayed at Oxford for about thirty years and it was in that university atmosphere that his ideas on education were germinated. Educationists are of the opinion that there was some inconsistency among his philosophical, educational and psychological, writings, but his contribution to educational theory and practice proved invaluable.

His *An Essay Concerning Human Understanding* and *Some Thoughts Concerning Education* disclose his views on educational theory.[21] *Some thoughts Concerning Human Understanding* contains his views on how to train the physical moral and intellectual aspects of the pupils. In his *An Essay* he emphasises on the issue of cultivating man's rational element. He believes that mothers and fathers are the most important directors, and after them carefully selected teachers.

In *Some Thoughts Concerning Education* Locke did not think to write about the education of ordinary people. He made it clear that he intended it as a guide to the education of young gentlemen. Secondly, his methods reflected in *Some Thoughts*, were intended for an individual system of instruction and not for the teaching of a large number of students in a classroom.

Locke formulated his education aims in three directions: (a) vigour of body, (b) virtue of soul, (c) knowledge or mental acquirements.[22]

As he was a medical doctor, he devoted his attention first to the care of the body. He warned parents against spoiling their children's constitution. He claimed that the strength of the physical body could be achieved only by gradual endurance of hardships which one gets in the course of life. He believed that a person could bear hardships to which from the beginning, he was used to. Keeping in view the point of enduring hardships, Locke strongly advised the parents that children should be taught to tolerate temperature change by not dressing too warmly either in winter or summer. He emphasized that they should spend as much time as possible in fresh air; should take baths in cold water and should sleep on hard beds. He insisted on simplicity of diet and advised parents to provide bread, milk and gruel during childhood. He had the sincere conviction that physical hardness was a prerequisite to the attainment of self-denial and self-restraint, both of which would become essential attributes in life.[23]

> "Plenty of open air, exercise and sleep, plain diet, no wine or strong drink, and very little or no physic, not too warm or straight clothing, especially the head and feet kept cold, and the feet often used to cold water, and exposed to wet".[24]

Locke attached more importance to the formation of virtuous soul and those social qualities which make a man reckon with 'good breeding' rather than simply to acquire knowledge. Locke thought that a sound mind need not mean a well-informed mind. A student may be good at philosophy, language and literature and at the same time he may not be considered an educated person. According to Locke learning was secondary but character, wisdom, virtue and breeding were primary.

Locke reflected in *Some Thoughts*: When 'a man is able to deny himself his own desires, cross his own inclinations, and purely follow what reason directs as best thought the appetite leans the owner way", he can be reckoned as a virtuous man.[25]

Locke did not agree to break the children's spirits by excessive discipline. He wanted them to realise right from infancy 'that there were things which they should and should not do'. He would like the children at ease and to be free but at the same time he would like them to be directed towards the right kind of things.

Coming to Locke's last aim of education, which is knowledge or mental acquirement, we find him totally disregarding the prevailing system of education in regard to both matter and method. He considered the contemporary education obsolete and condemned the study of the classical languages. But he wanted to retain the cultural, aesthetic and intellectual values of Greek and Latin literature.

As soon as the child begins to talk, the teaching of reading should begin, but it should be taught in a play-way manner. Only a few letters should be introduced at a time until the child learns the entire alphabet.

When the child begins to read, he should be given simple and interesting books to read. Locke recommended Bible stories to be provided to the children so that they may become interested in reading religion as well. Writing should follow reading.

Locke strongly favoured the study of the mother tongue from the very beginning. Once, when the child has learnt the vernacular, he could learn another language. The second language would be French. The method of instruction for all languages should be conversational. Normally, grammar should be studied when the students reach maturity.

Besides studying vernacular, students should also learn arithmetic, geometry and history. When the above subjects are learnt, astronomy and geography should also be included in the curriculum. Locke recommended the study of politics and government so that the students could have a good foundation of civil law. Since he wanted a gentleman to be good at social intercourse, he recommended dancing to be learnt by him. Locke considered dancing worthwhile because it could cultivate graceful movements and bring confidence. Fencing and riding, which were considered essential for good breeding, are recommended too. Finally, extensive travelling is also recommended by him as one of the best means to learning. Locke thought that the greatest means for social education was travelling, for it broadened the matured persons in a unique way. Locke also advised to include gardening and carpentary with the school curriculum, for their inclusion and practice would promote good health.

The programme for educating the gentleman, proposed by Locke, should end at the age of twenty. After that, he assumed, the young man would like to marry.

Locke included all those subjects for the training of the gentlemen keeping in mind the idea of utility criterion. Anything, which failed to fulfil the idea of the criterion, should be ignored from the syllabus.

Locke's Important Educational Ideas

Locke condemned the doctrine of innate ideas, which had been in vogue for centuries. He argued that if there were innate ideas all people should have them in common. He said that the only source for ideas was experience.

Since he rejected the doctrine of innate ideas, the *tabula rasa* theory was popularised. Locke contended that man's mind is passive and it can receive only the impressions made on it.

As a result of the introduction of the *tabula rasa theory,* two new educational points came to light before the modern educationists...

environmental determinism and equality among men. As Locke propounded that men began with nothing and there were no innate ideas, it led to that whatever they were to become they would become by their experiences. Thus, the importance of the environment was highlighted. If Locke was correct in putting forward his 'tabula rasa theory' or 'wax tablet analogy', then all men are created equal.

Considering that the chief purpose of education was to develop character, Locke strongly advocated the importance of private teaching and did not appreciate public education.

Looking back into Locke's ideas about curriculum studies, it becomes evident that he advocated the provision of only that kind of learning experience, which would bear the principle of utility. In this way, he emphasized an important fact which could not be omitted by the modern educationists at the time of curricular planning.

In his 'An Essay Concerning Human Understanding', he seemed to say that mental habits... for example, an ability to reason correctly, and the capacity to arrive at prudent judgment... were superior to information. He regularly insisted on distinguishing a sound and orderly mind from an informed one. With all this, it is certain that Locke preferred a mind which was able to think clearly, reason scientifically and judge correctly. This makes us think that he was formulating the theory of formal discipline, which later on became an important educational idealogy.[26]

Locke's position, by contributing such important ideas to the realm of education, becomes quite conspicuous. He has been variously classified by the educationists. He has been called a humanist, a realist, an utilitarian, an empiricist and an inventor of the theory of formal discipline.

REFERENCES

1. Boyd, *History of Western Education*, p. 239.
2. Crombie, Alistair C. (1959), *Medieval and Early Modern Science*, (New York: Doubleday, Garden City), Vol. II.
3. Power, *History of Education*, pp. 413-14.
4. Power, *History of Education*, pp. 413-14.
5. Clark George N. (1949), *Science and Social Welfare in the Age of Newton*, (Oxford: Clarendon Press), pp. 75-84.
6. Keatinge, M.W. (1931), *Comenius* (New York: McGraw Hill Book Co.), pp. 108-17.
7. Boyd, *History of Western Education*, p. 242.
8. Comenius John Amos (1896), *The Great Didactic*, translated by M.W. Keatinge (London: Adams & Charles Blacke).
9. Laurie, S.S. (1890), *John Amos Comenius* (Cambridge: Cambridge University Press p. 55.

10. Rusk Robert (Reprinted 1974), *Doctrines of the Great Educators*, (London: MacMillan), pp. 93-94.
11. Rusk, *Great Educators*, p. 95.
12. Rusk, *Great Educators*, pp. 95-110.
13. Power, *History of Education*, p. 428.
14. Power, *History of Education*, p. 429.
15. *Pampaedia*, a manuscript work in Latin by Comenius, later on translated in German, contains, Comenius views on the seven stages of schools. Quoted by Rusk in his *Doctrines of the Great Educators*, pp. 103-05.
16. Rusk, *Great Educators*, p. 110.
17. Francis Bacon (1944), *The Advancement of Learning and Novum Organum*, Revised Edition, (New York: John Wiley & Sons, Inc.).
18. Rene Discartes (1952), *Descartes' Philosophical Writings*, translated by Norman Kemp Smith, (New York: The MacMillan Co.).
19. Power, *History of Education*, pp. 417-18.
20. Power, *History of Education*, p. 441.
21. John Locke, *An Essay Concerning Human Understanding* (1838) Ed., Tegg & Sons, London, *Some Thoughts Concerning Education* (1934) edited by R.H. Quick, (New York: Cambridge University Press).
22. Power, *History of Education*, p. 444.
23. Power, *History of Education*, p. 444.
24. Locke, *Some Thoughts Concerning Education*, p. 26.
25. Locke, *Some Thoughts Concerning Education*, p. 27.
26. Locke, *Some Thoughts Concerning Education*, pp. 28-30.

CHAPTER-VIII

THE DAWN OF NATURALISM IN EDUCATION

The seventeenth century was the most active hundred-year period in the history of education. Most of the educational growth centred around Realism, which meant that curricula, methods and students were put in direct contact with reality regarding worldly matters. Comenius was the greatest educator of the age. Locke spoke clearly about a new approach to education and upheld the criterion of utility in learning. But during the eighteenth century, it was gradually perceived that the seventeenth century schools were little affected by the revolutionary ideas brought in by Comenius, Bacon and Locke. The last two decades of the seventeenth century were quite unreceptive to a real educational awakening. Therefore, the revolution, brought in by the potential educationists of the century, did not gather much momentum.[1]

Still, we may think of the seventeenth century as a transitional period, wherein ideas were brought quite near Realism. In fact, in a way a foundation was laid down which subsequently brought progress.

Early eighteenth century schools, which had been operating under the influence of the realistic ideology, were severely critized by men as they were full of weaknesses. The elementary schools were poorly equipped in most of the ways; their curricula was circumscribed mainly to reading, writing and arithmetic and no decent education was offered by them to their pupils. Besides, most common people could not attend any school for this or that reason. Most of the teachers were poorly prepared and were unfit for the classroom. Classes were ungraded and a large number of boys and girls were put together into the same classroom. Since there was no organised curricula, they studied whatever their teachers taught them.

The grammar or secondary schools were not better than the elementary schools, although their teachers were a bit better and the curricula were orderly in comparison to the elementary schools. Yet the school programme did not have much relevance to the life in society. Secondary schools were classical schools and were considered having a very low standard. Thus, the picture of education at the beginning of the eighteenth century was a bleak one.

It was, therefore, not out of place that a demand for better schools gradually gained momentum. In France, the Brothers of the Christian Schools upgraded elementary education. In England a 'charity school movement' came into operation with the goal of teaching reading, writing, Catechism and prayers.[2] Alongside, under the auspices of the Church of England the Society for promoting Christian knowledge was organised. It aimed at promoting Christian knowledge by teaching the Catechism. Very soon more than two thousand schools came into existence in England and Wales, where not only the ideology of the Catechism was taught but instruction in the elements of education were also given. When these schools started functioning well, the Sunday School movement came into existence in England. The idea of the Sunday School was to offer instructions in reading, writing and religion to all the children who could not attend schools during the week.[3]

In Germany, August Hermann Francke's elementary schools, boarding schools and teacher-training schools started getting recognition. Sometime during 1717, Frederick William I, the king of Prussia, appreciating the need for equal educational opportunity to the common people, promulgated a decree, which made attendance in the elementary schools compulsory in Prussia. The fact is that Prussia's example had far reaching effects in Europe. It provided some kind of justification for state control of education too. Besides, reforms were brought in to improve higher schools, colleges and universities. Before Frederick's decree was promulgated, higher education was hardly touched by any reformers. The decree brought indirectly a new light to higher education too, and what was done at the level of higher education in Prussia, influenced the tone of higher education in Europe.

In the first place, the curriculum of the universities in Germany became broader. The realistic movement of the seventeenth century also influenced some of the pedagogical reforms, which took place during the eighteenth century. The curriculum was, therefore, not only made broader, but was permeated with the spirit and method of science and modern philosophy. The acceptance of the doctrine of academic freedom was another significant influence of the movement. The principle of research and freedom... the freedom of the teacher to study and teach and of the students to study and learn was accepted as a fundamental foundation for university life in Germany. The old universities, which had been following the practice of lecturing on standard works, accepted the new method, which was to present the facts and interpretations of scientific findings in lectures and in seminars to help the students to consolidate what they had learned. Finally, the modern universities, following the German model, began to serve the rising spirit of nationalism. All the lectures in the modern university were delivered in the vernacular. The entire spirit of modern higher education centred around independence and progress. It was clearly being understood that the university should aim at serving mankind and not simply advancing knowledge.[4]

Enlightenment

During the eighteenth century Germany was one of the European countries, where practical educational reforms took place ahead of other countries. In the field of theoretical reforms in education, the honour goes to France, where innovations took place in the realm of pedagogy ahead of any other country. France became the scene of the Enlightenment, which brought further reforms in education in that country.

It would be a bit difficult to trace clearly the doctrines of the Enlightenment, yet it can be stated that it was a revolt against the established order. The Enlightenment was critical, individualistic and destructive in nature. "The bond, which held the men of the Enlightenment together in a kind of loose relationship, was not a bond of friendship, but an affinity of ideas—was the rejection of authority. It could be called anti-authoritarianism. Nothing that could be recommended by reason or common sense was accepted. The Enlightenment was critically rationalistic."[5]

One of the important figures belonging to the Enlightenment movement was **Rousseau,** who was born in Geneva in 1712. He went one step ahead of others. He did not remain content with glorifying reason which the others did but rejected reason itself. He attached 'reason' with such an intensity that he became a reformer of all the reforms which had been brought into by the Enlightenment.

Rousseau produced ideas which were not common to the eighteenth century educationists, who were stressing that education should have social objectives and the state should exercise its control on education to achieve such goals. Rousseau propounded a doctrine which contended that the purpose of education was to produce a man... not a political or a social or a special kind of man, but just a natural man. This thought brought a variety in the concepts of aims of education. Should then the goals of education be social or individual? It was Rousseau who stressed the importance of individual aims in education. He was soon joined by the other educationists of his age. **Condillac** (1715-1780) and **Helvetius** (1715-1771) contributed greatly to the line of thought Rousseau had reflected.

As educationists, both Condillac and Helvetius do not occupy a prominent position in the history of education but both expressed what have been called sensationalist views on education.

Condillac in his *Treatise on the Sensations* (1754), and Helvetius in his book *On the Soul* expressed that man's faculties have their foundations in the senses. Therefore, the first goal of the educator must not be the training of senses but the awakening of understanding and judgment. 'The mind is nothing more than the sum total of all of man's experiences. When one mind is better than another, this excellence is due to the quality and quantity of the experience it has had; any other interpretation affirming qualitative differences among men, is deplored mainly by Helvetius.'[6]

Condillac's and Helvetius' reflections made educational reformers think more and more of the influence that the social environment was having on the formation of character. They also began to realise that the development of men depends primarily upon opportunity, therefore, society should control the environment and offer a good environment and opportunity for a better development of man.

Apart from Condillac, Helvetius and Rousseau, there were other educationists who expressed their views on almost similar perspectives. After Rousseau had published *Emile*, **Louis-Rene de la Chalotais** (1701-1785) published his book, *Essay on National Education* which contained his plan for a national system of education. He did not place education in the hands of the religious people or the Church but argued that laymen should play a larger role in shaping the educational future of France.

La Chalotais' views on national education were not immediately accepted by the European countries, yet a wave of new ideas swept over Europe. In England, a few years after La Chalotais' reflections on national education, **Joseph Lancaster** (1778-1838) and **Andrew Bell** (1753-1832) put into effect a plan based on a national system of education. It was a plan for monitorial schools, which had a liberalizing influence on education. Although the quality of monitorial teaching was not very effective, its' appeal was financial. One teacher should be able to teach a large class. The schemes of education, propounded by Lancaster and Bell, did not really achieve much success, but their efforts made the public of England aware of the need for more and larger schools. Monitorial schools did not fail because their quality of instruction was poor, but because such schools became entangled with sectarian religion. After several years the monitorial school system collapsed in England, but it brought an awareness and appetite for a national system of education.

During the first three decades of the eighteenth century, Germany had made a considerable progress in establishing national education. The attendance of boys and girls in the schools had already been made compulsory by the royal decrees. The possibilities of national education were further realized by the efforts made by **Johann Bernard Basedow** (1724-1790).

Basedow was very much influenced by Rousseau's assertion that men learn through natural experience. He made efforts to put Rousseau's theory into practice by advising teachers to follow the correct method of teaching. Basedow's two shorter books, *The Elementary Book* and *The Book of Method* reflect his views on the practical business of managing schools. In 1774, Basedow published a full-length book, *The Elementary Work*. It contains his best thoughts on what should constitute a school's curriculum, and how best teaching methods should be used.

Basedow was very much interested in testing his educational theory in the real school situations. He tested some of his new ideas at the 'Philanthropinum', a school located in Dessau. By 1784, for personal or professional reasons, Basedow severed his associations with the new school but his influence in Germany and Prussia was felt most in the coming years.

One of the educationists, who was greatly influenced by Basedow's views on national education, was Prussia's **Baron Von Zedlitz,** who had been Frederick the Great's minister of education from 1771 to 1789. As minister of education in Prussia, he advanced the idea of national education by reorganizing the classical schools and promoting the scientific study of education. As a result of Von Zedlitz's encouragement, a university chair of pedagogy was established at the University of Halle in 1779.[7]

Von Zedlitz's sincere efforts to establish a national system of education in Prussia brought good results in Germany. After a couple of years from the time of the establishment of the university chair of pedagogy at Halle, Germany issued decrees which brought all colleges and schools directly under the control of the State.

In fact, the notion that 'all the institutions need to be controlled by the State' was shared by almost all the important educationists of the eighteenth century. Rolland expressed his views in this respect in his *Report;* Rousseau reflected such views in his, *Consideration on the Government of Poland;* Helvetius did so in his *On Man* and Turgot in his *Memoirs.*[8]

Jean Jacques Rousseau (1712-1778)

Rousseau was born on the 28th June, 1712 in Geneva. He came from a middle class-family of French Protestants. His mother died at his birth. For some time he was in the care of a parental aunt but there he learned nothing of restraint, self-denial or obedience. The absence of a mother in Rousseau's early childhood greatly affected his life. The lack of maternal care resulted in highlighting the role of motherhood in Book I of his *Emile.*[9]

Later on he was looked after by his father. When he was ten years old, he was sent to a tutor from whom he learnt Latin for two years. From that time onwards he lived a most unsettled life. He worked as an apprentice to an engraver for sometime, and then ran away from him. Then he tried to work as a tutor but was not very successful in that.

A long career of unemployment brought him a sense of frustration and unfulfilment. He started feeling bitterly about the society in which he lived. His life reached a crisis when, in 1737, he had a serious illness during which he began to read a variety of books on literature, philosophy and science. It was then that he read Voltaire, Montaigue and Descartes. He also read Pope, Addision and John Locke. He then started writing. He won a prize for a 'Discourse on the Arts and Sciences' in 1750. The essay was judged best by the Academy of Digon and was awarded by them. After this success, he wrote a number of essays and articles on general topics. He then started writing the main works of his career: *The New Heloise* in 1761, which was a romance of love and domestic life; *The Social Contract* in 1762, which provided the leaders of the French Revolution with their main ideas about government; and *Emile* in 1762, which was his chief work on education.[10]

Emile

Rousseau's *Emile* consists of his ideas which he finalized out of his own life's experience. He believed that the needs of educational reform include a return to nature, a development of the natural man and a simplification of the entire scholastic pattern. *Emile* was published when Rousseau was about fifty years old. The main theme of *Emile* was based on the proposed educational reforms which included the essential liberty of natural man. The book consists of five parts. Book I deals with the years infancy to age five; Book II, from age five to twelve; Book III, from age twelve to fifteen, Book IV, from age fifteen to twenty two.[11] Book V deals with the education of women. *Emile* is an example of education in action meant for a child selected for experiment. The child is Emile, who is educated in three ways: by nature, by things and by men.[12]

Rousseau's Theory of Education

Rousseau's views on educational reform are interwoven with his views of social theory. His aim of education is to make a person a unit, a whole being who could find himself in society. His theory of education is concerned with the direct and unconscious development of the individual whose natural growth is not thwarted by outer hindrances. He feels that education must perform both negative and positive functions. It must remove hindrances and provide experiences which help in developing a natural man.

The main thesis of *Emile* is that "everything is good... as it leaves the hand of the author of nature; everything deteriorates in the hands of man." The first sentence of Book I reads: "God makes all things good; man meddles with them and they become evil."[13] Rousseau reflects in *Emile* that man is moulded by society and the educational process must help to develop the child's autonomous tendencies without being subjected to authority.

Book I of *Emile,* which deals with the years of infancy to age five, describes how a child's life should be made simple and rugged. He assumes the two arts indispensable to life and happiness: self-knowledge and self-control. Then he discusses general things. He devotes a good deal of attention to who teachers should be, what they should know and what their relationship should be with students. He is a confirmed advocate of the tutorial method and emphasizes the importance of one pupil with one teacher, who always guides him rather than instructs, and whenever possible he withdraws to allow the pupil to learn for himself. Rousseau unquestionably prized learning by discovery and advocated the idea of freedom very emphatically.[14]

In Book II of *Emile,* where education from ages five to twelve is explained, he begins by stating that everything in traditional educational practice was bad and, therefore, needs to be rejected. He further states that the child's rights must be protected and he should be allowed full freedom to construct his own value judgment and frame his own personality.

Most important features of his theory of education are some of his reflections, which he made in Book II of *Emile.* He has some particular ideas for educating the child between the ages from five to twelve. He says: "Do nothing and allow nothing to be done." This is Rousseau's doctrine of negativism, which will be discussed separately in this chapter. Rousseau is of the opinion that unlimited freedom must be provided to the child to learn what interests him and has meaning for him.

In Book III of *Emile,* Rousseau lays down the criterion which would help intellectual education to develop and frame good character. For all that, three things would be important: necessity, usefulness and moral suitability. Rousseau thinks that whatever truth resides outside the context of necessity and use, should be ignored. Rousseau advises his readers, 'the great danger in life and education is not ignorance, for ignorance never harms anyone, but error, which, if allowed to go uncorrected, can be fatal.'[15]

Out of the three criterion, which are the charter for intellectual education, the principal one is use. Rousseau wants that the child should never be told anything he is unable to understand. He wants him to begin learning by cultivating a desire for learning. He emphasizes learning and how to learn more than merely acquiring knowledge. These are some of his fundamental principles of all good education.[16]

In Book IV, which contains educational principles for teaching children from fifteen to early twenty years of age, Rousseau is concerned with ethical and moral training. Rousseau thinks that to be moral means to act according to the dictates of one's heart. He wants moral teaching to begin with two great truths... God, and man's soul, which would lead to natural self-love and provide opportunity to conceive the right meaning of good and evil.

Rousseau reflects humanitarian inclinations and is deeply concerned about moral relationships among men. But he does not accept the importance of institutionalized religion. Rousseau is, perhaps, religious in a very broad sense and he wants Emile to be really religious, yet he wants him to stay away from churches. Morality could be formed naturally. It should begin with self-love. With his self-love, Emile should become selfish due to his natural inclinations to compare himself with others. Out of this selfishness, Emile begins to realise that all men are fundamentally alike. It would generate a love for human race. This love can be transferred into sound ethical action.[17]

Direct moral teaching finds no favour with Rousseau. Throughout *Emile* Rousseau has reflected that the education of children should take place away from society, which according to him is always filled with evil influences. During the period of social education Emile will find out his own weaknesses from his own experience. He will become moral in his own way, which would not be an outcome of the dictates of formal and organized religion. Rousseau wants Emile to be religious and moral but both attributes should be gained through natural consequences of right living.

Book V is mainly concerned with the education of girls. Rousseau thinks that in man and woman, nature has contrived to make two beings alike and at the same time different. Therefore, man should be strong and agile and woman should be weak and passive. Therefore, they are to be educated differently. A woman's education must be planned in relation to man. Rousseau thinks that 'woman is specially made for man's delight',[18] so women's education should make them pleasing in men's sight and make them win men's love and respect so that they could make their lives pleasant and happy.

In *Emile,* Sophy is the woman figure representing all women. She is Emile's perfect mate whom he meets somewhere in the countryside. Sophy is supposed to be a good-house wife, who is good at needlework, lace-making, cooking and house-keeping.

Rousseau's Negativism

Rousseau's education consists not in teaching virtue or truth, but in keeping the heart away from vice and from the spirit of error. Emile learns discipline by natural consequences. There are neither direct or indirect moral lessons.[19] Emile must taste life as it is and must know about illness and suffering.

Rousseau advises parents and teachers to love children, to encourage them and to indulge them in their sport. The foundation for the best education is not to gain time but to lose it.[20] Rousseau does not want Emile to learn through text books, except one... *Robinson Crusoe,* which is allowed as it contains a treasure of natural education.

The positive education of the childhood period comprises physical and sensory training. The physical education is more or less modelled on that of Sparta. Regarding sensory training, Rousseau is of the opinion that feet, hands and eyes are to be trained first. But training the senses does not, however, mean practising formal exercises. It implies judgment by their means in concrete situations encountered in life. For example, he proposes such tasks as determining whether a ladder is big enough to reach the cherries on a tree and whether a plank is long enough to bridge a stream.[21]

This is how Rousseau wants Emile to be self-reliant and self-sufficient. Emile, through natural education becomes a good social being. There is no place of churches or institutionalized religion in Rousseau's *Emile,* yet he wants Emile to be religious through the examples he learns as a means of natural consequences. *Emile* is certainly Rousseau's great work on education and is a forerunner of a most natural theme in the threshold of education.

John Heinrich Pestalozzi (1746-1827)

Pestalozzi was born at Zurich on January 12, 1746. His father died when he was very young, so his mother brought him up with great hardships.

Pestalozzi's school career was quite an unhappy one. He neither had many good friends nor did he enjoy the school environment, as he often became the prey of his school-master's jokes.

It was almost by accident that Pestalozzi later on became a professional teacher although his own schooling had prepared him for the ministry, which he accepted for a brief time, working as a pastor.

From the beginning of his career as a pastor, he always tried to seek the means to achieve the betterment of mankind. Whenever possible, he tried to reflect upon Rousseau's naturalism and showed a clear interest towards his humanitarian inclinations.

Some time during his early life, Pestalozzi read Rousseau's *Emile* and became ardently attached to his doctrines of educational reform. As he was too much influenced by Rousseau's educational reforms, he accepted his doctrines of natural education. In order to implement Rousseau's doctrines in a practical way, Pestalozzi bought a farm on which he opened a school to conduct it on Rousseau's principles.

From the beginning of his career in the field of education, Pestalozzi engaged in writing books and pamphlets on various topics. He wrote the most important work, *Leonard and Gertrude* sometime in 1780. Its first part was published in 1781. The second part was published in 1785. The first part of the book describes a village community in which so many of the lower class people live. Throughout *Leonard and Gertrude* Pestalozzi maintains the importance of sympathy and desires to provide justice to the poor. He also emphasizes the importance of mother's love, which is depicted through Gertrude. These are some of Pestalozzi's fundamental reflections of his theory of education.

The second part of the book consists mainly of the list of the various kinds of injustices that were in vogue at that time. He also wrote the third part of the book, which prescribes the remedies to improve the poor conditions of the lower class people. Like Rousseau, Pestalozzi believes in reforming the society. But first of all, he wants the old fashioned schoolmaster replaced by a smart and agile young lieutenant. Then he reflects that the school must provide a wholesome environment which should be in the closest connection with the life of the home and not in contradiction to it.[22]

Leonard and Gertrude is an educational novel, which has a story of the old-fashioned schoolmaster. Soon he is replaced by a young lieutenant, who is a disabled war veteran. The lieutenant begins his work against filth, laziness and disorder. There are forty young children, who do a great deal of manual work and receive instructions in this direction. Teaching methods are greatly emphasized. A good order, without harshness, is maintained. Children are encouraged to develop good habits and helped to learn through what they see and hear, for senses are considered important to receive real knowledge.[23]

After completing the fourth and the last part of *Leonard and Gertrude*, Pestalozzi had the satisfaction of conveying all what he had desired to do. *Leonard and Gertrude* is a didactic novel, which describes how ideas can be practised and how the schoolmaster can become practical in the right sense.

Pestalozzi's Teaching Techniques

Pestalozzi is especially interested in those teaching techniques which may cultivate the powers of attention, observation and memory. He wants the children to draw, write and work while they learn. He believes that sound is the first elementary means of instruction. Therefore, he collects a set of combination of syllabus which the children repeat aloud. This type of approach was almost similar to the phonetic approach with which he managed to teach his pupils effectively.

Pestalozzi's own book, *How Gertrude Teaches Her Children*, contains the importance of the first impression of objects or sense perceptions, which he thinks are the basis for our knowledge. He thinks that if laws of learning are followed, education could become a science. So, he classifies the knowledge gained through sense impressions into three concepts; number, form and language. Pestalozzi puts all this in the following manner.[24]

"When a confused conglomeration of objects is brought before our eyes, and we wish to dissect it and gradually make it clear to ourselves, we have to consider three things:

(1) how many things and how many kinds of things there are before our eyes i.e. their number;
(2) what they are like i.e. their form; and
(3) what they are called i.e. their names."

Pestalozzi wants children to learn each object both as a separate unit in itself and as a member of a family of related objects. The study of words should also follow the same pattern.

Pestalozzi's teaching techniques influenced the later educationists to a great extent. They started stressing teacher-preparation and grading the objects and lessons so that learning and teaching would be more effective and lasting.

REFERENCES

1. Power, *History of Education*, pp. 453-56.
2. John W. Adamson (1964), *English Education 1789-1902*, (New York: Cambridge University Press), pp. 132-33.
3. Joseph Strafford (1880), *Robert Raikes and Others, The Founders of Sunday Schools*, (London: Sunday School Union), pp. 15-33.
4. Power, *History of Education*, pp. 458-59.
5. Power, *History of Education*, pp. 460-61.
6. M. Grossmen (1926), *The Philosophy of Helvetius*, (New York: Teachers College Press), pp. 152-53.
7. Fredrick Paulsen (1906), *German Universities and University Study*, (New York: Charles Scribner's Sons), pp. 179-80.
8. Power, *History of Education*, pp. 470-71.
9. Jack H. Brrome (1963), *EMILE*, Translated by Barbara Foxley, (New York: E.P. Dutton and Co., Inc.), pp. 115-21.
10. Morrish Ivor, *Disciplines of Education*, pp. 82-83.
11. Rousseau Jean Jacques, *Emile*, translated by Barbara Foxley, 1938, (New York: E.P. Dutton & Co., Inc.), pp. 128-72, 321.
12. Power, *History of Education*, pp. 476-77.
13. Rousseau, *Emile*, p. 5.
14. Power, *History of Education*, p. 478.
15. Power, *History of Education*, pp. 481-82.
16. Rousseau, *Emile*, p. 135.
17. Power, *History of Education*, pp. 483-84.
18. Rousseau, *Emile*, p. 322.
19. Rusk, *Great Educators*, pp. 184-85.
20. Rousseau, *Emile*, p. 134.
21. Rusk, *Great Educators*, pp. 186-87.
22. Pestalozzi Johann H., *Leonard and Gertrude*, Translated by Evachanning, 1906, (Boston: D.C. Heath and Company), p. 118.
23. Power, *History of Education*, p. 492.
24. Pestalozzi Johann H., *How Gertrude Teaches Her Children*, Translated by Lucy E. Holland & F.C. Turner, 1915, (New York: C.W. Bardeen Syracuse), p. 47.

CHAPTER-IX

THE RISE OF SCIENCE AND NATIONAL EDUCATION

It was the beginning of the nineteenth century when the rise of science and national education began to be perceived quite distinctly. In fact, seeds of national education had already been planted in the later half of the eighteenth century. The nineteenth century simply witnessed its seedlings sprouting and flourishing.

The Industrial Revolution, which had already started, brought changes in the economic field. It also affected the social structure of most of the European countries. The French Revolution, which started during the second half of the eighteenth century, had greatly influenced the political structure of Europe and a new political philosophy containing strong notions of liberty, equality and fraternity started coming over the horizon. These words—liberty, equality and fraternity had profound meaning and unusual appeal. Therefore, both their meaning and appeal affected the destinies of education. To provide greater opportunity for the individual was now not considered enough, but more than that it was the demand for national education, which became the focus of attention of the people during the nineteenth century. It resulted in providing a better shape to the national school systems controlled by the State. In the movement for national systems of education, the desire of the people for an education with some religious perspective, was also retained.

With all sorts of influences carried forward from the eighteenth century, the nineteenth century developed some distinctive characteristics of its own. They were nationalism and democracy. Besides these two, another important aspect of the European life was distinctly witnessed. It was a strong drive to overthrow the clericalism which had been influencing the lives of the people for centuries. Thus, with these three characteristics, nationalism, democracy and anticlericalism, the new century made strides in all directions and influenced the educational thought and practice as well. In the national system of education democratic tendencies came into clearer focus during the century. The champions and educational leaders, who pushed the democratic thoughts into educational practices during the nineteenth century, were Johann Friedrick Herbart and Friedrick Wilhelm August Froebel.

Johann Friedrich Herbart (1776-1841)

Herbart was born in Oldenburg, Germany in 1776. His childhood was spent in the care of his mother. He received elementary education from the local paster and secondary education in the local Gymnasium.

Since his father was interested that he should study law, Herbart entered the university of Jena to study law. But he was not very interested in the law. Gradually, his attention was turned to philosophy and education. It was somewhere at that time that Herbart came in contact with Schiller, who was writing his letters on the Aesthetic Education of man at that time. It is said that this book created a great deal of interest in Herbart towards education.

He left the university of Jena in 1797 and after some time he met Pestalozzi. By that time, Herbart had already gathered much from Pestalozzi's writings and experiments and had laid some of the foundation for his educational theory. He was now ready to follow his own road.

His good academic career at Jena brought him many fine private assignments of teaching. He was also made professor of philosophy and pedagogy at the University of Konigesberg in 1809. By this time, his views on education had already been matured and he began writing on philosophy and education.

Herbart's Theory of Education

As a philosopher, Herbart accepted the view of the "soul" or the mind that had been offered by John Locke sometime previously. Herbart, like Locke, considered mind to be a *tabula rasa* in its original position and thought that all ideas were the products of time and experience. His educational doctrines seemed to have been greatly influenced by such philosophical formations. Some of the following books by him contain his educational principles:

> *The Application of Psychology to the Science of Education, Letters and Lecture on Education, The Science of Education;* etc.

Considering the importance of education, Herbart desired that these principles should be a perfect integration of theory to practice and a starting point for any theory of education should be the 'nature of man'. He advised students to study psychology, which could also provide the basis for making the teaching techniques more scientific. Herbart is one of the leading figures in the field of history of education, who laid the foundation for a scientifically oriented teaching methodology. He also established an institute for men and women to train them in the techniques of teaching based on scientific principles.

Herbart's Aims of Education

Herbart thought that the goal of education was the production of good men. In his book, *The Science of Education*, he reflects: "The one and whole work of education may be summed up in the concept of morality".[1]

Although during Herbart's university education, the emphasis was laid down on the growth of intellect, he thought that production of a good and moral man was of a greater concern to education. It was Herbart's impression that 'the worth of a man is measured by his will and not by his intellect'. He would have the educator, who is not necessarily the teacher or the instructor, but one who goes to make up the good man.[2]

Herbart conceived morality of being made up of 'five moral ideas': freedom, completeness, goodwill, right and equity.[3] 'Education, in this way, showed the aim of making a man who could know what he ought to do on every occasion and how to do it. It should be concerned with giving him the bases of instruction so that he could be a broad man; and this was the teacher's task. It would be a matter of cultivating in him the right ideas with respect to what we today call brotherhood. Education would, in addition, have the job of establishing in the individual an attitude that regularly respected the rights of others, both their persons and their property. Finally, there was the moral idea of equity. The educational assignments was to inculcate the idea of regard for good behaviour and punishment for bad or evil behaviour. The man, who could gather these five moral ideas and had made them part of his system of values, was a good man according to Herbart.[4]

Herbart's Teaching Methods

Herbart's methodology rests on experimental psychology. For that kind of approach, he tried to develop a scientific pattern.

One of the important elements of psychology, which Herbart considered important for his teaching methodology, was 'interest', which he thought was important for the attention of the learner. If the teacher wants to utilize certain ideas for the development of the child, he must create interest in him so that the new ideas get predominance over the others. This is all part of the conditioning process. The interests of the child are put into a certain frame of reference, and certain ideas or habits of action are derived from them. New experiences are made to fit into the background of these past experiences and become part of a performed frame of reference. Manipulating interest, then, was for Herbart an important part of the educative process.[5]

For pedagogical purposes, Herbert classified interests into two categories: interests that had to do with nature and interests that had to do with society. That is, interests that had to do with the physical world wherein the child lived, and interests which arose regularly from the social world in which he also lived. Neither of the sources of interest could be neglected while educating the child.

The Herbartian teacher must understand the role played by interest in the teaching-learning situations. Besides, he should be concerned with three more things when he begins to teach his pupils. They are: to relate the new lesson to what the child already knows; to help him to retain what has been taught; and to seek to maintain a high level of interest in the student, not only for what is currently being learned, but for learning in general. All this means that teaching and learning are dynamic processes.[6] This leads us to five Herbartian steps of instructions.

It is said that the famous Herbartian steps of instruction were the creation of Herbart's disciples and not his own. The five steps are: preparation, presentation, association, systemization and application.[7]

Herbart's scientific approach to education influences the world of pedagogy to a considerable extent. These pedagogical principles affected Germany first, where teachers and school directors paid attention to his definitions of educational aim, morality and his psychological conceptions of mental activity. These five steps of instruction were widely accepted as one of the best approaches in teaching methodology. In fact, Herbart is one of the first educators who accelerated the pace of science education in the modern educational world.

Friedrich Wilhelm August Froebel (1782-1852)

Froebal was born at Obesweissbach in Central Germany. His father was a pastor. His mother died when he was only a year old. Since his father remained too busy with his church duties, young Froebel was left to the care of his brothers and servants. His step mother didn't take much interest in him after the birth of her own son. Later on an uncle tried to provide him opportunities of education, but he left him too, considering that Froebel did not have much interest in education. For sometime he was apprenticed as a forester but at seventeen he left that job too.

It was sometime during 1799 that Froebel want to the University of Jena to visit his brother. It was then that he desired to join the University to recover the lost time. He enrolled in the University but there too his stay was short. From there he changed from one position to another, and finally accepted the position of a drawing teacher in Frankfort Normal School, which was being operated on Pestaluzzian principles. It was at that time when Froebel was with this institute, that he realized that his preparation for teaching needed a more substantial scholastic background. At the same time he seemed to realize that there was a dimension to teaching and learning that had not yet been fully exploited. He began to see that the method of teaching must be directed by the laws of development of the human mind as well as by those of the subject to be taught. This principle, that the method of teaching and the child's development should go hand in hand, became the central theme in his pedagogy and he was determined to exploit the idea fully.[8]

In order to bring more reforms to education, Froebel considered it necessary to pursue further education for his own growth. So, after he had stayed with the normal school at Frombefort for more than two years, he joined the universities of Gottingen and Berlin. Froebel did remarkably well in his university studies despite the fact that his early educational career was full of impediments.

After the Napoleonic wars, Froebel settled in Berlin and started experimenting his new ideas on a group of twelve students in 1817, at a place called Keilhau. He remained with the Keilhau school until 1831 and went to Switzerland. Before he left for Switzerland he had published his book *The Education of Man,* which contained his formal views on education. It was in 1840 that he opened the Universal German Kindergartens and devoted himself to the progress of such institutions throughout Germany for more than twelve years.

Froebel's Philosophy

In order to know Froebel's ideas on the theory of education, let us examine his philosophy first as it had a strong bearing on his educational views.

On the philosophic plain, Froebel maintains idealistic traditions. Unity is Froebel's dominant principle. All things are selected, connected, unified, whether or not this unity can be noticed. The final source of the unity or the principle of all unifications is God. The whole purpose of education is to enable men to fulfil and to complete themselves, and to attain unity with God.[9]

Besides his principle of unity, he conceives that the world has developed out of the process of organic evolution. Both men and plants have grown out of a similar kind of process, except that the plants, including animals, develop according to a strong inner law of their nature; man, being endowed with a mental nature, is able to shape many of the elements of his own development.[10]

Froebel considers each stage of man's development important and the principle of unity, according to him, flows through all the various stages of development.

Froebel's Theory of Education

Self-activity

Like most educators Froebel is concerned with the aims of education too. Froebel conceived two-fold aims of education. One of them is to produce a moral being and the other is to develop a good social being. In short, Froebel was expressing the view that education's main task should be moral and social.

Froebel believes that there are definite periods of a child's development. These periods should go hand in hand with the educational experiences based on self-activity. He means by this that all kinds of learning should take place while the child is involved in self-activity. Therefore, the curriculum should be made up of those activities and experiences which could lead the child towards the strength of character.

Play

One of the important steps in leading the child to maturity is play. It is the most characteristic activity of the childhood period. Froebel considers play as the highest phase of child-development. At this period it is a self-active process of the inner-representation which springs from the inner necessity and impulse of the child. Play, says Froebel, is the purest and most spiritual activity of man and, at the same time, typical of human life as a whole. It gives, therefore, joy, freedom, contentment, inner and outer rest, peace with the world. It holds the source of all that is good. To have educative value, the play of the child must be a purposeful activity. These play impulses must be directed and controlled by using definite material presented before him in an orderly manner so that homogeneous development takes place in him.[11]

Froebel believes that childish activity degenerates if it is aimless or not properly directed. In the Kindergarten the children are guided to bring out their plays in such a way that they help to serve for their development. Froebel, unlike Rousseau, suggested that human activity needed guidance without which there could be no free development.

Direct Contact with Nature

Froebel did not believe in bringing the child to the realms of nature in the way Rousseau would have liked. But he was quite convinced that nature-study must be part of the school curriculum. His school programmes included weekly excursions into the fields in order to bring children nearer to nature. Literary studies which would be related to nature and mathematical studies, which involved men measuring or describing nature, were the good examples presented by Froebel in relation to nature study.

School to Provide Social Education

It was Froebel, who for the first time reflected that school could play an important role in advancing human relations. Formerly school was considered a place where only intellectual or moral activities could take place. But Froebel's Kindergarten was a place where social education was provided for the children. This kind of role of school was unknown to the educators before Froebel.

Kindergarten

Froebel's most important contribution to education is his kindergarten. The kindergarten is a place where children grow, develop and learn in a most natural way. His first kindergarten was established in Blankenburg in 1837. From Germany the kindergarten spread to different parts of the world in a few years of time.

Thus, Herbart and Froebel are the greatest contributors of the nineteenth century. Herbart can be referred to as the father of the science education as his accomplishments in educational psychology are great. Froebel founded the kindergarten which has been his most important contribution to education.

The Growth of National School Systems

The large educational movement of the nineteenth century was mainly concerned with national education. Different countries of Europe began to see the relationship between education and national life. National systems of education first achieved its highest development in Prussia. Then it spread to Germany, France and England.

The work of Herbart and Froebel started getting recognition and the great European countries began to undertake the work of reorganizing their school system on the patterns suggested by these two leading educationists of the nineteenth century.

GERMANY

Though Prussia had been defeated by the Napoleon army and it had less freedom to launch any new experiments for its development, the field of education was still receiving great attention by the Prussians through the efforts of **Johann Gottlieb Fichte** (1762-1814). Fichte chose to concentrate on education as an instrument for social and political reforms and led the German states to accept this new role of education to achieve both social solidarity and national awakening. Gradually the German states, through their newly discovered educational system, achieved the essential social foundation for national unification, which in return generated patriotism and love for the fatherland.

The most important aims of education besides the intellectual and moral pursuits, were now to provide educational opportunity and to prepare persons for life in society. **Wilhelm Von Humboldt** (1767-1835), who remained as the minister of education for little more than a year, encouraged people to embrace the newly founded educational system. Von Humboldt's greatest achievement was the establishment of the University of Berlin. It was almost at this time that the idea of academic freedom started getting more attention from the people. The University of Berlin was granted full liberty to manage its own affairs connected with study, teaching and its administration. Soon the Berlin University set standards of excellence in scientific investigation which were gradually followed by other German universities. Gradually, German higher education began to wear a new face and more German universities became research orientated.[12]

Along with the growth of higher education towards a national system of education, German secondary education also developed to a great extent. The old classical courses were abandoned and in their place broader instructional programmes, which could meet society's needs, were developed. Traditional secondary schools known as Gymnasiums, were reorganised. Besides the Gymnasiums, two types of German secondary schools were developed in the nineteenth century. They were known as Realgymnasium and Oberrealschule. All three types had certain common characteristics; they admitted boys only; twenty years of age was the normal age for graduation in all types of secondary schools; and all taught German, history, music, religion and physical education.

Changes took place in the elementary German education too. Educational objectives were reconstructed and elementary education was made free and public; attendance in schools was compulsory from ages six to fourteen and great care was taken in the selection of teachers, who were mostly men. Broad aims of elementary education were allegiance and devotion to the nation.

FRANCE

Only a few things are worth mentioning about the growth of education in France during the nineteenth century. Education in France had been controlled by the state from the time of Napoleon, so it was not a new phase of education in France. But after the second half of the nineteenth century had passed, not much was done to improve education in France. National leaders became concerned about the educational opportunities for the common men. So **Victor Cousin** (1792-1867) was commissioned by the state to prepare a report on what could be done.

The work of Cousin led the French government to make the Primary School Law of 1833, which made educational opportunities available for common men both at primary and higher primary schools. It directed all such schools to conduct a curriculum which consisted of French, reading, writing, spelling, grammar, composition and arithmetic. Religion was taught to the children if their parents approved it.[13]

By the last quarter of the nineteenth century, under the careful administration of **Jules Ferry** (1832-1893), who also served as a minister of public instruction for four years, education in France became a state function and was completely guarded by the State. It was being considered a vehicle to achieve national goals.

ENGLAND

Like France, England also did not witness much as regards its educational development during the nineteenth century. Still the Industrial Revolution had brought many changes in English life. Many directives and acts were passed which had direct or indirect effect on education. The act of 1833 prohibited the employment of children under nine years of age and two hours instruction each day was made compulsory for children between the ages of nine and thirteen. By 1870 England had made enough progress towards a national system of education, which required all children to attend elementary schools.

There are two important educationists who belong to the nineteenth century in England. They are: **Robert Owen** (1771-1858) and **Herbert Spencer** (1820-1903). Owen was one of the most popular figures of the century. The infant school was his best known effort at reform. The infant schools were elementary schools which offered educational opportunities to poor children between the ages of five and ten. In fact, Owen generated a great deal of sympathy for the poor and reflected a great humanitarian outlook, which was very much needed in England at that time.[14]

Herbert Spencer is not much known in the educational history of England as a contributor to the cause of national systems of education. Instead, he is known as an educationist, who highlighted the cause of science education. According to him it was scientific knowledge which was more important for the growth of the individual. Thus, Spencer completed the educational traditions, which had been started by Rousseau and Pestalozzi.

Almost at the end of the nineteenth century the English government established a commission known as the **Bryce Commission** (1895). This Commission recommended a public system of elementary and secondary schools. It was obviously a conspicuous milestone on the progressive road of a national system of education in England.

RUSSIA

It was **Alexander II** (1855-1881), who was responsible for starting a national system of education in Russia. He established a state system of elementary schools which were open to all children, though attendance was not made compulsory. Before Alexander II, Catherine created a Commission in 1786 for the establishment of schools. The Commission's recommendations brought many changes to the educational system in Russia. Primary schooling was tuned to a two-year course consisting of reading, writing, grammar, arithmetic and religion. Curricula in higher and private schools were broadened. But in 1855, when Alexander II came to power, he directed for up-grading and opening new schools so that educational opportunities could be provided for all.

By the beginning of twentieth century, Russia freed itself from the clutches of the past traditions and brought into being an entirely a new system of education which became national, both in spirit and practice.

REFERENCES

1. Herbart Johann F. (1908), *The Science of Education: Its General Principles Deduced from Its Aim, and The Aesthetic Revelation of the World*, translated by H.M. and E. Felkin, (Boston: D.C. Heath and Co.), p. 57.
2. Power, *History of Education*, p. 502.
3. Herbart, *The Science of Education*, pp. 28-30.
4. Power, *History of Education*, pp. 502-03.
5. De Garmo Charles (1904), *Herbart and Herbartians*, (New York: Charles Scribner and Sons) pp. 88-101.
6. Power, *History of Education*, p. 5.7.
7. Herbart Johann F. (1901), *Outline of Educational Doctrine* translated by A.F. Lange, (New York: The Macmillan Co.), pp. 69-75.
8. Hughes James L. (1904), *Froebel's Educational Laws for All Teachers*, (New York: Appleton-Century-Crofts, Inc.), pp. 115-18.
9. Froebel Friedrick (1892), *The Education of Man*, Translated by W.N. Hailmann, (New York: Appleton-Century-Crofts Inc.), pp. 69-71.
10. Power, *History of Education*, p. 513.
11. Power, *History of Education*, pp. 512-15.
12. Baroness B. Von Marenholx-Bulow (1895), *Reminiscences of Friedrich Froebel*, (tr) by Mrs. Horace Mann, (Boston: Lee & Shephered), pp. 66-68.
13. Power, *History of Education*, pp. 517-18.
14. Power, *History of Education*, p. 527.
15. Smith Frank (1931), *A History of English Education 1760-1902*, (London: University of London Press), pp. 75-91.

CHAPTER-X

THE DEVELOPMENT OF DEMOCRATIC AND PRAGMATIC EDUCATION

The Growth of American Education in the Twentieth Century

The changes brought into the educational arena during the nineteenth century were felt more ardently during the first two decades of the twentieth century. During this time, education on all levels became more popular—specially on the American soil.

From 1890 to the outbreak of the Second World War, a tremendous growth of education on all levels was recorded. During this period a regular increasing percentage of the school-age youth of America was attending school. The increase of enrolment in high schools and colleges was at a phenomenal rate. By 1918 all the American states had compulsory-attendence laws which made universal education a reality. The schools were given more financial aid and the salaries of the teachers were almost doubled. By 1930 the percentage of population in schools reached 67 per cent and the school year was increased from 135 to 172 days. The education ladder extended from the primary school through the university. Americans could claim now that they had almost a perfect democratic system in education, which was extended equally to both privately owned and government controlled schools.[1]

The struggle for equal educational opportunity for all kinds of American citizens had been going on for a long time. The question of equal opportunity had two dimensions: first, the extension of opportunity in all directions; second, the opening of schools to all the children of all people without regard to race, creed or colour. Both dimensions were of great importance for the future growth of education in America. As a result of the Americans' ambition to provide equal opportunity for the citizens, many government decrees and acts were proclaimed from the third to the fifth decade of the twentieth century. But with the enactment of the Civil Rights Act of 1964, the black citizens became legally free to enjoy the full privileges of citizenship, though illegally segregation continues to exist in many states regarding education, housing and employment opportunities.

In order to provide maximum educational opportunity to all citizens, the American educational system was developed into a new dimension during the twentieth century. Now there were four new steps for the educational ladder: nursery schools, the kindergarten, the junior high school and the junior college, which later on was commonly known as the community college.

American Educationists

American educators were greatly influenced by the pedagogical reforms brought in by Pestalozzi, Herbart and Froebel. But the study of these European educationists led the American educators to develop their own pedagogical ideologies. Not only were the American educators able to develop independent pedagogical principles, but were now in a position to prepare a generation of their own educators. One of the important educators of repute was **Francis W. Parker** (1837-1902), who introduced a method, which was known as the Quincy Method. The general idea contained in the Quincy Method was that the old-line formal learning in the school should be replaced by a system in which learning and living should go hand in hand. This sort of system or practice later on was known as 'progressive education'. Thus, Parker was one of the first American educators who brought innovations to the American educational tradition. After Parker, the other American educator of great repute was **John Dewey**, who not only cultivated what Parker had invented, but brought in radical changes in the existing educational system which soon fell apart from the orthodox procedure. Let us now examine Dewey's philosophy and educational ideals in some detail.

John Dewey (1859-1952)

John Dewey was born in Burlington, Vermont, in 1859. His father was a shopkeeper in a small village. He attended the public school in Burlington to receive early education and proceeded to the University of Vermont where he graduated in 1879. In 1880, he went on to Johns Hopkins University to read philosophy, psychology and history. In 1882 he received his Ph. D. and accepted an appointment at the University of Michigan to lecture in philosophy. His wide abilities and his energetic approach to most of the current problems led to his appointment as

Professor of philosophy at the University of Minnesota and then subsequently at the University of Michigan.[2]

Dewey's Philosophy

The term 'pragmatism' is associated with the names of John Dewey, **William James** (1842-1910) and **C.S. Peirce** (1839-1914). In fact the term pragmation was first employed by C.S. Peirce to ascertain the meaning of a formula or an abstract idea. To Peirce pragmatism was a logical method which could be applied to mathematical and scientific problems. In very general terms when Peirce used the term pragmatism, he was considering more precisely the relationship between our conception of an object and its practical effects, and he saw in our conception of these effects the whole of our conception of the object.[3] But it was not a pragmatic test of truth. Rather it was the way of analysing the subject-object relationship. Dewey was not interested in using the term pragmatism in the way it was used by Peirce. He started thinking on the issue in a different way. In his own thinking Dewey began to abolish the distinction between ends and means. He thought that 'end' was simply a name which we gave to a series of acts taken collectively. The means was a name which he gave to the same series taken distributively. It was not the 'end' which mattered, since in absolute terms it could never be reached. In relative terms, each means was equally an 'end'. It all depends upon the point of view then.

Dewey did not reckon the realism of 'absolute truths' and 'ends'. He sought, enthusiastically, to explain everything in terms of 'growth' and 'evolution'. As a relativist he wanted to examine carefully the 'means' we used, for, he thought, the 'means' were 'ends' too. He emphasized the personal and variable element in things. According to him the truth or falsity of human inquiry depended upon its success or failure, and in its results for the individual himself. Dewey's theory of truth is usually referred to as instrumentalism. Knowledge is never an end-in-itself, it is always a means; it is a personal matter and each individual uses it for the purpose of adapting himself to new problems, new situations and new involvements. The meaning of any concept depends upon its relationship to the individual and his using thoughts, concepts and truths, in order to find personal solutions to his everyday problems.[4]

Therefore, the criterion of truth in any situation thus becomes the pragmatic test, which is considered in terms of satisfactory or unsatisfactory result. Curtis and Boultwod referring to Dewey's Instrumental Theory of Truth' point out:

"even scientific laws are but generalizations which may be modified again and again—they remain true only as long as they summarize truly the current state of human knowledge".[5]

Scientific laws are no more than current descriptions of observed mathematical averages and as our experience of the universe grows and our observations are analysed, the description of the scientific laws is also modified. Thus, Dewey, through his 'Instrumental Theory', reflects upon the nature of truth. He reduces all 'truths' to the scientific level of causation, which means that a thing is true if it 'furthers our purpose' such descriptions of truth are open to many objections. If we accept Dewey's statements that the test of truth lies in the consequences to which it leads, we are led towards scepticism. Again, if his pragmatic idea of 'furthering our purpose' means truth, it may lead to a sense in which something may be true for us at any particular moment, because it furthers our purpose. That reduces the meaning of 'truth' to something meaning a 'provisional utility'. But 'truth' certainly cannot be defined in such terms. Dewey's description of the meaning of the term 'truth', therefore, has some of the above referred limitations. Still, his philosophy formed as a basis for a progressive form of education which will be considered hereunder.

Dewey's Views on Education

Dewey's philosophical position was that of pragmatism, while his educational principles were pragmatic in nature. This theory of education was an outcome of his philosophic reflections.[6] The Laboratory School at Chicago, which was opened in 1896, was an attempt to experiment with his educational principles. Dewey himself could go to the laboratory and experiment and continually made use of the experimental method.

From the very beginning, Dewey was much influenced by Froebel's educational ideals. Like Froebel, Dewey also saw the problems of education in their social setting. He visualized the school as a nursery for the citizens of the future. The central theme for the child education was a concept of creative self-expression, in which children lived out their experiences in all their activities. In his book *The School and Society*, Dewey summarizes the principal educational views in the following manner.[7]

(i) The main business of the school is to train children to be co-operative and helpful to each other. The school must develop in them the consciousness of mutual interdependence and ability for adjustment.

(ii) All sorts of educative activities should be investigative and induced by impulsive attitude rather than an application of external material. All spontaneous activities of children should be used for educational purposes.

(iii) The individual tendencies and activities of the children are organised and directed in such a way that they may be used later on for the benefit of the society they are finally going to live in.

The kind of school Dewey had in mind was one which could produce people for complete living in the world of today. He regarded the school like an ideal home or like a large family or a living community involved in different kinds of activities, which were of interest to all the children who were all partners in a common effort. Each had something of importance to contribute to the success of the whole.[8]

For Dewey the school was a place for living. It was a place where each child could learn to discipline himself through experience. In order to enrich that experience Dewey accepted the need for a teacher, who could understand his individual pupils and provide the right suggestion at the right time. Dewey was of the opinion that the teacher must realise that the influences experienced by a child are all important. Therefore, the children must fully apprehend the meaning of experiences and learn how to communicate.[9] The teacher's role is to engineer situations and arrange experiences wherein communications are possible.

Dewey strongly objected to the subject-based curriculum. He thought that subjects were simply summaries of human activities. Therefore, children should reach them by making a summary of their own experiences. These subjects are useful to adults for they are the storage of knowledge, but children are not yet ready for that sort of analytical approach to their world and cannot know the subjects as the adults can. In his book, *The School and the Child,* Dewey reflects that the child is the standing-point. He is the centre for all the activities and he is the end. His development and growth are the only 'ideal' that Dewey would allow.

In his *Democracy and Education,* Dewey states that the child's experience is useful, significant and even true contextually. There are no absolutes and there are no ends, remote or immediate. The educational process has no end beyond itself. It is its own end. It is a process 'of continual reorganizing, reconstructing, transforming'. Dewey believes that education is growth and its purpose is to encourage moral, mental and physical growth.

Thus, the purpose of the school becomes more important and its role, according to Dewey, is more pragmatic. Dewey and his followers termed the school in the direction of affinity with real life situations. This new direction described education as a matter of 'teaching students not subjects', but 'educating the whole child.' Education is not a preparation for life, but it is life itself.

As a progressivist Dewey borrowed ideas from Rousseau, Pestalozzi, Herbart and Froebel. Induced by new ideas, Dewey challenged the education of the past as well as the education of the present in a nember of important books, some of which have been referred to under this section of Dewey's educational ideas. Their chronological order of publication is as under:

School and Society, was published in 1899; *How we Think,* in 1909; *Democracy and Education* in 1916; *Human Nature and Conduct,* in 1922; and *Experience and Education* in 1938.

Besides these books Dewey also wrote hundreds of articles. The main purpose of all his writing was to create the new educational tradition which was backed by formulating a new theory of education. The other important educationist, besides Dewey, who tried to create a new educational tradition was William James.

William James (1842-1910)

William James was born in New York in 1842. His father was a mystic, this mysticism was well combined with wit and humour. The son inherited all the three qualities from his father. After some sessions in American private schools, William was sent to study in private schools in France, where his brother Henry also obtained education.[10]

After a few years of his school education William pursued medical studies and took his M.D. at Harvard University in 1870. He took up teaching at Harvard in 1872 and taught there until 1910 when he died. During his long stay at Harvard he wrote a number of books and articles. His greatest achievement was almost his first book—*The Principles of Psychology* (1890). It contains a unique mixture of anatomy, philosophy and analysis. In it he defined philosophy as 'only thinking about things in the most comprehensive possible ways'.

After 1900, the number of his publications increased quite conspicuously. His *The Will to Believe* had already been published in 1897. His next book was *Varieties of Religious Experiences,* which was published in 1902. His most famous book *Pragmatism* was published in 1907; *A Pluralistic Universe* in 1909; *The Meaning of Truth* in 1909; and *Some Problems of Philosophy* in 1911. His last book, *Essays in Radical*

Empiricism was published two years after he died i.e. in 1912.

Jame's Pragmatism

James always directed his thoughts towards things. As a mirror of external and physical reality, the old atomistic belief, which conceived thought as a series of separate ideas mechanically associated, was condemned by James. He reflected: 'Thought is not a series, it is a stream, a continuity of perception and feeling, in which ideas are passing modules like corpuscles in the blood.'[11]

James reflected that consciousness was not an entity. Neither it was a thing, but a flux and system of relations. Consciousness was a point at which the sequence and relationship of thoughts coincided with the sequence of events and the relationship of things. Such moments were the moments of reality itself. There was, therefore, no need to go beyond the experience process to a soul.

After reading an essay, "How to Make Our Ideas Clear", published in the *Popular Science Monthly,* written by Charles Peirce, James found a lead to follow. He tried the problems and ideas of the old metaphysics by the test suggested by Peirce. They fell to pieces like chemical compounds when they were shot through with an electric current. This led James on to new definitions of truth. So far the metaphysicians conceived 'Truth' as an objective relation, as once good and beauty had been. James thought, 'what if truth were also relative to human judgment and human needs?' He reflected that 'all sorts of truths are formulations of experiences which are convenient and successful in practice. Truth is simply the 'cash-value' of an idea'. Men accept or reject things and ideas according to their needs and their temperaments and not according to objective truth.[12]

Such candid reflections and pragmatic thoughts brought a great revolution in the realm of men's thinking. Educational reforms and its theory and practice were bound to be affected by such revolutionary ideas. Let us now examine the theory of education propounded by these American pragmatists.

American Theory of Education

During the nineteenth century American educators did not pay much attention to educational theory. They thought that more than theory they needed school buildings, money for development and qualified teachers to meet the demand of increasing student-population. Whatever theory they needed, could be imported from abroad. As a result of lack of interest in developing a new theory of education, the American educators gladly accepted the views of Locke, Pestalozzi and Herbart. But this acceptance did not occur for a long time. The European educational theory had developed out of a different kind of social background and needs. The social system, which existed in America during the late nineteenth and early twentieth century, demanded quite a different kind of educational system. There was a great need of democratic type of education, which could provide equality of educational opportunities. Besides, the Americans were also interested in extending universal opportunity for schooling to all their citizens irrespective of colour, creed or race. A new educational theory was, therefore, quite imperative.

The foremost educational philosophers in America were John Dewey, William James, and to some extent, Charls Sanders Peirce. Though Peirce's contribution to educational theory was small, the basic idea of pragmatism was extended by him. He reflected: "To determine the meaning of an idea, put it into practice in the objective world of actualities, and whatever its consequences prove to be, these constitute the meaning of the idea." Such a reflection influenced James and Dewey a great deal and they expanded Peirce's idea into a formal philosophical system, which later on was introduced to the educational realms.

With Dewey, pragmatism adopted a naturalistic outlook. Dewey's approach to the pragmatic—principle was different from that of William James, who had been willing to accept that the idea once tested had a degree of permanency. But Dewey regarded truth as relativistic. This line of thought had a great meaning for education. With such an outlook, Dewey conceived school as a social institution having social objectives. With this new educational theory the purposes came to dominate all others. School's main function was not the inheritance of the past but rather to put the student in direct relation with the society in which he lived. He needed to learn things not by reading about them but by living with them. For this the school environment must foster an informal environment consisting of the educational process which the student needed to learn. Thus, the objectives of education could not be listed in advance but were to be formulated as the children lived and learned in the schools.[13]

In the development of educational theory in America, Dewey and his followers form a group, which we call 'progressives'. Those who opposed the ideas and practices of Dewey and his associates are called 'essentialists'.[14]

The Essentialists

There were two kinds of essentialists representing two different sorts of essentialistic movements. One kind of essentialism was represented by **William C. Bagley** (1874-1946), a professor of education at Columbia University, Teachers College, Bagley. Professor Bagley's group organized effective opposition against the progressive education movement. The other kind of essentialism advocated a return to the fundamentals in education. They agreed on one issue that a common core to basic culture consists of the essentials of cultured life, therefore, this common core must be communicated in all the schools. This latter essentialistic group was divided into many small groups which advanced different educational theories, namely, idealism, realism, rational humanism and Christian humanism.[15]

The progressives were quite aware of such opposition groups. In order to prove that their progressive ideas were important, they organized the Eight-Year study. This was an attempt to prove the superiority of the kind of education they were advocating. A report was made on the Eight-Year study, which contained good arguments for it. The essentialists, however, were not much influenced by such progressive innovations. They still emphasized that the central theme of education must be to transmit cultural heritage and to achieve intellectual discipline. Besides, the essentialists such as James D. Koerner of the Council of Basic Education were of the opinion that extra curriculum must be placed in a subordinate position in schools in comparison to the main curriculum. James B. Conant, Arthur E. Bestor and John Wild reflected that students in high school should follow a common core of standard studies—English, social studies, history, government, mathematics, natural sciences and electives. Academic courses may be elected by good students and vocational or semi-vocational courses may be offered by less talented ones.[16]

Thus, the essentialists, from the early twentieth century, have been stressing that what is essential can be known and popular democratic education consisting of high quality is possible. Their contention is that knowledge or truth can be possessed and good human values can be contained and transmitted as well.

With all these educational developments taking place in America, education throughout the world has been reawakening to the hopes and needs of human beings. In this connection the efforts done by the United Nations must be noted, especially that of the UNESCO (United Nations

Educational Scientific and Cultural Organisation). UNESCO was founded in London in 1945. With 'Education for Peace' as its main ideal, UNESCO has been trying to spread information and to promote intellectual climate to bring peace to the world.

REFERENCES

1. Power, *op.cit.*, pp. 584-85.
2. Morrish Ivor, *Disciplines of Education*, p. 104.
3. Morrish Ivor, *Disciplines of Education*, pp. 107-08.
4. Morrish Ivor, *Disciplines of Education*, pp. 109-10.
5. Curtis, S.J. and Boultwood, M.E.A. (1965), *A Short History of Educational Ideas*, (U.T.P. 4th Edition), p. 463.
6. Dewey John (1916), *Democracy and Education* (New York: Macmillan) Chapter XXIV.
7. Dewey John (1900), *The School and Society*, (Chicago: University of Chicago Press), Chapter V.
8. Morrish Ivor, *Disciplines of Education*, p. 118.
9. Mead, G.H. (1934), *Mind, Self and Society*, (Chicago: University of Chicago Press), p. 79.
10. Durant, *Story of Philosophy*, p. 509.
11. Durant, *Story of Philosophy*, p. 510-11.
12. Durant, *Story of Philosophy*, p. 511-14.
13. Dewey, J., *Democracy and Education*, pp. 156-165.
14. Power, *History of Education*, pp. 603-04.
15. Power, *History of Education*, p. 604.
16. Power, *History of Education*, p. 605.

CHAPTER-XI

THE GERMAN TRADITION AND THOUGHT IN EARLY TWENTIETH CENTURY

The Advent of Existentialistic Movement

After the close of World War II in 1945, reports began to come in from Europe and America that a new philosophical movement was creating enormous excitement, particularly in Paris. Its leaders were not university professors of Philosophy but men who had produced novels, plays and philosophical treatises. The chief figures were said to be **Jean-Paul Sartre** and **Albert Camus**. The movement was called Existentialism.

As the movement started getting its roots firmer in Europe, many American thinkers responded with impatience as the themes of discussion proposed by the Existentialists were irritating to them. Anxiety, homelessness, death of God and sentimental longing for the past things, which were considered as the central facts of man's condition by the existentialists, were dismissed by the Americans as they thought that it was a post war phenomenon which simply reflected irrational over-reaction on the part of such European thinkers who had been leading Existentialism.

But, the truth was that by the end of the 1960's it was made clear that Existentialism was not merely a post war reaction of the 1940's, but it marked one of the great central traditions in thought as well as literature of the century. And with the passage of time it became a part of the established modern cultural life. After 20 years from its start it did not circumscribe chiefly as a French phenomenon as German thinkers like **Martin Heidegger, Karl Jespers** and **Friedrich Nietzsche,** the **Jewish** theologian **Martin Buber,** French Roman Catholic philosopher **Gabriel Marcel,** Danish thinker and theologian **Soren Kierkegaard,** also joined the movement.[1]

Existentialists' Main Concern

It would rather be difficult to enlist the details about Existentialistic movement and thought in this small work but essential thoughts, which run as the main under-current in the movement, will be recorded to highlight the movement.

It is the passion for life which seems to be the first motto of the existentialists, but as we read on we experience deep despair hidden in their writings. Life for the existentialists, is full of conflict and contradiction from which no human being is ever free. Therefore, man must make room for conflict and contradiction in his life.

The existentialists are certain about the fact that men are finite, their preoccupation with the past is intense and it is the future which decides whether the past is living or dead.[2] Man himself is at the highest point of reality, but there is also a real world, which with all the power and substance is ready to swallow him up. Man has intelligence and freedom to protect himself against all the odds and to guide his own destiny. Nothing else is there. The existentialists reckon that when man experiences the physical world first time, he is always in danger of being overwhelmed by the fact of experience itself. Although experience is powerful, it is all on a non-reflective level. As man grows and matures, he becomes more reflective about his experience and consequently has a better chance for controlling the agencies of nature.

Existentialists condemn determinism as they consider it man's greatest enemy and approve freedom which they take as man's best friend. Therefore, belief in freedom must be cultivated along with the belief and sense of responsibility. This is the greatest message to education by the existentialists.

Man as a creature is locked up within his own loneliness and solitude which influence man's thoughts and hinder him from the understanding of truth. Therefore, man's principal attention, with all serious reflection, must be man himself. The important thing, in short, is not the abstract universality of any system of objective ideas, for reality is too 'slippery' to be caught by such a net. The important thing is that how one finds sustaining one's life—and the only sort of truth that really matters is a truth which is 'existential', which is 'subjective', a truth that one has earned and which is, therefore, one's own.[3]

Yet another important theme or main concern of the existentialists is that 'man faces an alien universe, therefore, he needs to achieve an *authentic life*. And with the notion rampant that basically man experiences uncertainty and insecurity, there is little chance for him to survive at all occasions unless he can summon *adequate courage*. But *courage* is a virtue which is attained with great difficulty. Therefore, it is quite likely that man may be tempted to try to escape the right direction leading to truly *authentic life*. He may then divert himself to the routines and customs what Kierkegaard called 'the public', and finally fall into deep despair.

It could be true that the attainment of authenticity may not be possible until we as humans are not brought up short against the great limiting realities of *suffering* and *guilt*, or *sorrow*, *disappointment* and *death*. For it is then only when man feels the sting of failure or when hopes have been shattered, he starts appreciating human finitude. Therefore, without any experience of extremity and without the necessary equipment of wisdom and maturity no real authentic life can be attained.[4]

At this juncture it would be necessary to make a mention of some of the above referred existentialists who stand apart from others and whose contribution to the existentialistic movement is immense.

Soren Kierkegaard (1813-1855)

Soren Kierkegaard who is commonly regarded as the father of modern existentialism, is also the first European philosopher who bears the existentialist label. His work is too diffuse and voluminous to add to this humble book. Keirkegaard had a strict religious upbringing and seemed to have been bothered by a sense of family guilt, which gradually dragged him to develop a melancholy disposition. At the age of twenty-three he was already writing of himself in his journal as 'inwardly torn as under' and 'without any expectation of leading a happy life.'[5] It is, therefore, not surprising that the notion of individual or the exceptional man would come to him as a major thought. He reckoned that subjectivity and intensity should be prized as the criteria of truth and genuineness. Accordingly, the reality is touched in the intense moments of existence, mainly during moments of painful decision.[6]

For quite a long time Kierkegaard remained occupied with the religious problems and with how to become a Christian. He considered that the progress of the human-self was from the aesthetic through the ethical to the religious stage but again it could not be rationalized or presented in a logical manner. Kierkegaard later on reflected that Christianity itself was the paradox and demanded the leap of faith. What commonly considered for Christianity—the doctrines and ceremonies of conventional Church was a perversion. Towards the end of his life Kierkegaard became quite violent in his attacks on Christian institutions.

In his last Journal he criticized that Christianity could simply be known in world-renouncing terms and as the inward decision of the individual. The New Testament, Kierkegaard reflected, had to do with man's will and every expression said 'forsake the world, deny yourself, die to the world, so hate oneself, to love God and so on'.[7] His two books, *Philosophical Fragments* translated by David F. Swenson in 1936, and *The Concept of Dread*, translated by Walter Lowvie in 1944, are worth recording.

Kierkegaard had no immediate successors. Neither his work was esteemed much in the nineteenth century. Yet his ideas, which were deeply involved with the existentialistic spirit, started appearing in different forms little before his death. In this line of thought, who could be considered next to him, was Friedrich Nietzsche.

Friedrich Nietzsche (1844-1900)

Friedrich Nietzsche like Kierkegaard, was of religious background, born of a clerical family. His sensitivity of mind almost ended in madness. Most of the time, except during last few years, Kierkegaard was preoccupied with becoming a Christian, but Nietzsche was obsessed with getting away from Christianity. Nietzsche considered Christian faith as a 'continuous suicide of reason.'[8]

Much has been written about the 'death of God', 'God is dead', 'God remains dead'. And we have killed him' by Neitzsche in his *Joyful Wisdom* which was translated by Thomas Common in 1910. His *The Will to Power*, translated by Ludovici in two volumes, published in 1909, created a great turning in the minds of the Nazis and it is said that much of the Second World War was hatched out of such ideology.

Karl Jespers (1883-1969)

Nietzsche's anguish and frustration could not drive people for a long time. Karl Jespers almost broke out from Nietzsche's tradition and thought. He began his career as a psychiatrist and soon became interested in what he termed as 'limit situations' of life. But such situations opened to us the reality of *Transcendence*. His voluminous writings, mainly *General Psychopathology*, translated by J. Hoenig and M.W. Hamilton, published in 1963 at Chicago and *Man in the Modern Age*, translated by Eden and Cedar Paul, published at London in 1933, explore the relations between the human existent and the world, on one side, and between the existent and *Transcendence* on the other.

Martin Heidegger (1889-1976)

Martin Heidegger's major work *Being and Time,* translated by J. Macquame and E.S. Robinson in 1962, first published in German language around 1927, is considered his most impressive analysis of 'human existence' in the existentialistic movement. The prominence of themes such as, care, anxiety, guilt, finitude and death in Heidegger's writings is taken as indication of a trend towards a kind of nihilism. That kind of impression was further strengthened by his famous inaugural lecture given at Freiburg in 1929 on the theme, "What is metaphysics?" It was in this lecture that Heidegger reflected that metaphysics had to do nothing.[9]

Among the lasting influences on his thinking was the phenomenology of Husserl, an interest in the question of 'being' and his preoccupation with language, which he attributed to the period he spent in a Jesuit Seminary. It was also observed that he had interest in the writings and thoughts popular before the age of Socrates. With his own trend of thought, which leaned more towards nihilism, he gradually disassociated himself from the humanistic existentialism of Sartre. His other noteworthy work is *What is called Thinking?,* which was translated by F.D. Wieck and *J.G. Gray* in 1968.

Martin Buber (1878-1965)

Martin Buber was one of the best among existentialists who had interpersonal approach. This Jewish philosopher was quite different in his existentialistic outlook in comparison to the others. Other existentialists tended to concentrate on the problem of man's relation to the world; sometimes on his relation to God or Being. Buber was more interested in man's relations with each other and strongly believed that there cannot be an existent apart from his relation to other existents. This is also reflected from his number of books which he wrote to express his strong beliefs. Among those, *Between Man and Man,* translated from German by R.G. Smith in 1955, *I and Thou,* translated by Smith in 1958, and *The Knowledge of Man,* translated by M. Friedman in 1965, are the best known books depicting existentialistic philosophy on the issue of interpersonalship.[10]

Jean-Paul Sartre (1905-1980)

Jean-Paul Sartre French existentialist remained close to Nietzsche in various aspects of thinking. Sartre conceived that man himself had to take the place of God. He reflected: 'Man's being condemned to be free, carries the weight of the whole world on his shoulders; he is responsible for the work and for himself as a way of being'.[11]

But Sartre, like Nietzsche, indulged with the dark side of the situation of freedom for he reflected that man's desire to be God was essentially self-contradictory and frustrating. Sartre believed that man had no fixed essence given in advance, neither he was a manufactured thing. Both Nietzsche and Sartre including Camus, saw human existence transcending into the nothing.

Among Sartre's famous books are: *The Emotions: Outline of a Theory,* which was translated by B. Frenchtman in 1948, *Existentialism Is a Humanism,* edited by Walter Kaufmann Being and Nothingness, translated by H.E. Bernes in 1956 and *Nausea* translated by Lloyd Alexander in 1959.

Gabriel Marcel (1889-1973)

Before mentioning Marcel we would like to say a few words about **Albert Camus** (1913-60). Camus developed a kind of existentialism which is described as an 'anti-theist' rather than an atheist. For Camus, Sisyphus was the symbol of ancient hero who was condemned to spend his rest of the days at the top of a hill, who tried to escape many a time but crashed back down at the bottom.[12]

Gabriel Marcel is one of the best known French existentialists who was against the pessimistic elements which could be observed in Sartre and Camus. He, in fact, offered 'Metaphysic of hope' which is mainly reflected in his book Homo Viator translated by E. Craufurd in 1951, and which contains a sense of human community. In this respect he confronts individualistic tendencies projected by Sartre in his writings. Marcel's other important book is *Being and Having: An Existential Diary,* translated by K. Farrer in 1949.

The Existentialistic Theory of Education

The existentialists always considered 'human freedom' very important. They, therefore, concluded that whatever destiny man carved out of himself, was upto him. He was always in a position to choose one thing or something else but he must choose something. No man or woman was absolved from making something of himself or herself.

As man strives to make something of him, help is needed. The help comes from education. Therefore, education, besides making the concept of freedom known to man, should also help to make him something. Schooling, which gives knowledge, is quite important for the existentialists as it is through it that man can achieve what he wants to be.[13]

The school is basically a place for having experience with life, for existentialism as well as pragmatism reject the so-called spectator theory of knowledge. Therefore, schools should try to immerse their students in life but with proper caution, for the existentialists attitude towards knowledge 'radically affects the teaching of those subjects which are dependent upon system of thought or frames of references: it states that school subjects are only tools for the realization of subjectivity.'[14]

Most of the realization of subjectivity, which is another way of saying fulfilling one's personal goals, is just to adopt a set of values or a code of conduct according to which personal life will be lived. Values, according to existentialists, are not something which man is authorised to own or to reject but they are inevitable and imperative. Whether these values are sets of values lodged in the legacy of the race or some society, or whether they are drawn from the nature or supernatural law, makes not much difference. The source of values is not of much consequence, for personal endorsement is required to these (some) values. Values, existentialists reckon, are translated from the objective to the subjective realm by an act of personal choice which under no circumstances can be avoided. Although man is free to choose his moral code, but by the very nature of his existence he can never refuse to choose some moral code. It should not be taken that the existentialists are heading towards determinism, which in any case, they reject. It is just a natural functioning of man's life to choose some values. Life is an entirely personal game and as man grows, the rules of the games are determined.[15] In this making of life, where personal choices are imperative, educational experiences are of great importance as they influence man's thinking and knowledge.

Besides the fulfilment of personal goals, freedom and responsibility are yet another important aspects of existentialists. They consider everyone to be free to go to his own way. But if that is true, how then education can be of much help. The person, who chooses a value, is in the moral position to choose what he perceives to be an ideal. But the best education prepares him to *will* his own freedom as well as the freedom of others and make him assert the value of any action with universal appeal. As Sartre reflects: "I am responsible for myself and for all." To provide or develop that responsibility should be the role of education. Therefore, to follow the above line of thought it can be concluded that an existentialist teacher is a missionary for freedom and responsibility and not merely a school master who is simply concerned to teach a curriculum. His role is to protect and preserve the pupil's academic freedom and help develop his *will* to choose good values for life. On the part of the student it is imperative that he develops himself as a rational being. With freedom of choice and responsibility for what he chooses, he keeps a commitment to fulfilling his personal goals. As such, the purpose of education is to provide an extensive and comprehensive experience with life in all its forms. The existentialists like pragmatists, also propose liberal education with no fixed teaching methods. Only that method is good which provides happiness and good character.[16]

An Evaluation

Although existentialistic philosophy brought a new dimension of thought and stressed upon the importance of man's existence, freedom and responsibility, there are opinions which are detrimental to the existential philosophical position. Let us consider some of them.

One of the complaints against this philosophy is that existentialism is irrational in its tendency. The rejection of reason finds its most elaborate modern expression in the voluminous writings of Kierkegaard. Closely related to the charge of irrationalism is that of amoralism. Both these charges can be refuted if we try to go deep into the existentialistic philosophy. Existentialism at its best is neither irrational nor anti-rational, but is rather concerned with affirming that the fullness of human experience breaks out of the confines of conceptual thought and that our lives can be diminished by a too narrow rationalism. Similarly, the issue of amoralism can be condemned as the existentialists state that if man is to claim for himself the moral freedom, that can only be acceptable if there go along with it a heightened sense of responsibility and a more penetrating ethical analysis which will highlight some norms.[17]

Next to the above two points of criticism there are two other charges against existentialism. One of them is that existentialism is infected with an undesirable degree of individualism, and at the same time, a closely allied complaint that existentialism is a subjectivism. But Buber and Marcél break out of a narrow individualism into a theory of intersubjectivity. Besides, most existentialists take the existence of the individual as the starting point and when this first step has been taken into consideration, perhaps the bias towards the existence of the single individual could be well understood.[18]

The other charge is that existentialism is too narrowly humanistic in its outlook. But considering the fact that existentialists are surely interested in the well-being of man, the above charge could not be acceptable. Besides the above charges, existentialism is said to be pessimistic and even morbid. Its philosophers and adherents are said to be blind to the promise of the contemporary world. There may be some truth in these charges but the man-centredness of existentialism had surely provided us a thrust towards technological exploitation. And even though the existentialists may have been greatly negative in their outlook towards the world, we would have to acknowledge that they have pointed out before us the real evils and dangers which affect man's existence.[19]

Just like any other philosophy, existentialism has its weaknesses too. But if seen dispassionately, it would be clear that its merits outweigh its weaknesses. Existentialism has projected many fresh ideas which could be considered as penetrating insights into the mystery of our own human existence. As a consequence it has contributed to the protection and growth of humanity against the threats which lurk today towards the individual. More than that as John Macquarrie remarks: "From existentialism we can learn truths that are indispensable to our condition and that will be essential to any sane human philosophy of the future."

REFERENCES

1. Nathan A. Scott, Jr. (1969), *The Unquiet Vision: Mirrors of Man in Existentialism.* (New York: The World Publishing Company), pp. 13-17.
2. Sartre Jean-Paul (1956), *Being and Nothingness* (Tr.) Hazel E. Bernes, (New York: Philosophical Library).
3. Nathan Scott, *The Unquiet Vision*, p. 31.
4. Nathan Scott, *The Unquiet Vision*, pp. 31-32.
5. Kierkegaard Soren (1954), *Journals* ed. and Trans. Alexander Dru, New York, p. 40.
6. Macquarrie, John (1972), *Existentialism*, (New York: Penguin Books), p. 54.
7. Soren Kierkegaard (1965), *Journals*, 1853-55, ed. R. Gregor Smith, New York, p. 266.
8. Nietzsche, Friedrich (1959), *Beyond Good and Evil*, trans. Francis Golffing, Chicago, p. 46.
9. Macquarrie, *Existentialism*, p. 57.
10. Macquarrie, *Existentialism*, p. 58.
11. Sartre Jean-Paul (1956), *Being and Nothingness: An Essay on Phenomenological Ontology*, trans. Hazel Barns, (New York: Philosophical Library).
12. Macquarrie, *Existentialism*, pp. 58-59.
13. Power Edward J. (1968), *Philosophy of Education*, (New Jersey, Prentice-Hall, Inc.), p. 143.
14. Kneller George F. (1958), *Existentialism and Education*, (New York: Philosophical Library), p. 63.
15. Edward Power, *Philosophy of Education*, pp. 143-44.
16. Edward Power, *Philosophy of Education*, pp. 144-45.
17. John Macquarrie, *Existentialism*, pp. 276-78.
18. John Macquarrie, *Existentialism*, pp. 279-81.
19. John Macquarrie, *Existentialism*, pp. 280-81.

BIBLIOGRAPHY

Aristotte, (1941), *Basic Works,* (ed.) R. McKeon, (New York: Random House)

Aristotte, *Politics,* VII.

Bacon, Francis, (1944), *The Advancement of Learning and Novum Organum,* Revised ed., (New York: John Wiley & Sons, Inc.)

Baron, Hans, (1966), *The Crisis of the Early Italian Renaissance,* (Princeton: Princeton University Press)

Bolgar, R. R., (1954), *The Classical Heritage and Its Beneficiaries,* (London: Cambridge University Press)

Boyd, W., (1964), *The History of Western Education,* (London: Adamsand Charles Black)

Bowen, James, (1972), *A History of Western Education,* (London: Methuen & Co.)

Bury, J.A., (1922), *A History of Greecs,* (New York: St. Martin's Press)

Chadwick, O., (1958), *Western Asceticism: Selected Translation* (London: SCM Press)

Chaster G. Starr, (1968), *The Awakening of the Historical Spirit,* (New York: Alfred A. Knopt, Inc.)

Clark, George N., (1949), *Science and Social Welfare in the Age of Newton,* (Oxford: Clarendon Press)

Comenius John Amos, (1896), *The Great Didactic,* (tr) M.W. Keatinge, (London: Adams & Charls Blake)

Crombie, Alistai, C., (1959), *Medieval and Early Modern Science,* (New York: Doubleday, Garden City).

Curtis, S.J. and Boultwood, M.E.A. (1965), *A Short History of Educational Ideas,* (U.T.P. 4th Edition).

Daly, Lowrie J., (1961), *The Medieval University,* (New York: Sheed and Ward).

Davis, W. S. (1923), *Life of a Medieval Barony,* (New York: Harper & Row).

Daniel, D. McGarry, (1954), *Renaissance Educational Theory* (History Bulleton U.S.A.)

Dewey, John, (1916), *Democracy and Education,* (New York Macmillan)

Dewey, John, (1900), *The School and Society,* (Chicago: University of Chicago Press)

Durant, Will, (1970), *The Story of Philosophy,* (New York: Washington Sq. Press)

De Garmo, Charles, (1904), *Herbart and Herbartian,* (New York: Charles Scribner and Sons)

Descartes, Rene, (1952), *Descartes' Philosophical Writings,* (tr.) Norman Kemp Smith, (New York: The MacMillan)

Eby, Frerick, (1931), *Early Pròtestant Educators,* (New York: McGraw Hill Book Co.)

Enhard, (1960), *Life of Charlemagne,* (Michigan: University of Michigan)

Fowler, W.W., (1925), *The Roman Festivals of the Period of the Republic,* (New York: Macmillan)

Fredrick, Paulsen, (1906), *German University Study,* (New York: Charles Scribner's sons)

Friedenthal, Heinrich, (1946), *Road to Reformation,* (Philadelphia: Muhlenberg Press)

Froebel, Fridrick, (1892), *The Education of Man,* (tr.) W. N. Hailmann, (New York: Appleton—Century—Croft, Inc.)

Gwyn, Aubrey, (1926), *Roman Education from Cicero to Quintilian,* (New York: Oxford University Press).

Grossmen, M. (1926), *The Philosophy of Helvetius,* (New York: Teachers College Press)

Heinrich, Boehmer, (1946), *Road to Reformation,* (Philadelphia: Muhlenberg Press)

Herbart, Johann F., (1908), *The Science of Education: Its General Principles Deuced from Its Aims and Aesthetic Revelation of the World,* (tr.) H.M. and E. Felkin, (Boston: D.C. Heath & Co.)

Herbart, Johann F., (1901), *Outline of Educational Doctrines* (tr). A. F. Lange.

Hugo of St. Victor, (1961), *Didascalican: A Medieval Guide to the Arts,* (tr.) Jerome Taylor, (New York: Columbia University Press)

Hughes, James L., (1904), *Froebel's Educational Laws for All Teachers,* (New York: Appleton-Century Crofts, Ino)

Hyma, Albert, (1930), *Erasmus and Humanism,* (New York: F. S. Crofts & Co.)

James, J. Auchmuty, (1937), *Irish Education,* (Dublin: Hodges, Figgs & Co.)

Jack, H. Borrome, (1963), *Emile* (tr.) Barbara Foxley, (New York: E. P. Dutton & Co. Inc.)

John, W. Adamson, (1964), *English Education*, (New York: Cambridge University Press)

Joseph, Strafford, (1880), *Robert Raikes and others of Sunday School,* (London: Sunday School Union)

John, Hghus W., (1935), *A Brief History of Ancient Times,* (London: Ginn & Co.)

Jowett, B., (1928), *The Republic of Plato,* Third ed. (tr.) Q.U.P.

Keatinge, M.W., (1931), *Comenius,* (New York: McGrew Hill Book Co.)

Kierkegaard, Soren, (1954), *Journals,* (ed. & tr.) Alexander Dru, New York.

Kneller, George F., (1958), *Existentialism and Education,* (New York: Philosophical Library)

Laurie, S. S., (1903), *Studies in the History of Educational Opinion from Renaissance,* (New York: Cambridge University Press).

Leach, A.F., (1915), *Schools of Medieval England,* (London: Methun & Co. Ltd.)

Lewis, Campbell, (1962), *Plato's Republic*, (London: John Murry)

Locke, John, (1838), "An Essay Concerning Human Understanding", (ed.) Tegg & Sons London; "Some Thought Concerning Education" (1934) (ed.) R. H. Quick, (New York: Cambridge University Press)

Mason, J.E., (1935), *Genttefolk in the Making,* (Philadelphia: University of Pennsylvania Press)

Mancschreek, C. L., (1958), *Melanchthon, The Quiet Reformer,* (New York: Abingdom Press).

Macquarrie, John, (1972), *Existentialism,* (New York: Penguin Books)

Mead, G. H., (1934), *Mind, Self and Society,* (Chicago: University of Chicago Press.

Morris, Ivor, (1976), *Discipline of Education,* (London: George Allen & Unwin Ltd.)

Nathan, A. Scott, Jr., (1969), *The Quiet Vision: Mirrores of Man in Existentialism,* (New York: The World Publishing Co.)

Nietzsche, Friedrich, (1959), *Beyond Good and Evil,* (Tr.) Francis Golfting, Chicago.

Origen, (1957), *Contracelsum,* (tr.) Henery Candwick, (Cambridge: Cambridge University Press)

Pestalozzi, Johann H., (1906), *Leonard and Gertrude,* (Boston: D.C. Heath & Co.)

Pestalozzi, Johann H., (1915), *How Gertrude Teaches Her Children,* (tr), Lucy E. Holland and F.C. Turner, (New York: C.W. Bardeen Syracuse)

Plato, (1964), *The Republic,* (Penguin Books: Pelocan)

Poole, R. L., (1940), *Illustrations of Medieval Thought and Learning,* (New York: The Macmillan Co.)

Popper, K. R., (1966), *The Open Society and Its Enemies; The Spells of Plato,* 5th ed., (London: Routledge)

Power, Edward, (1970), *Main Currents in the History of Education,* (New York: McGrew Hill Co.)

Power, Edward, (1968), *Philosophy of Education,* (New Jersey: Prentice-Hall Inc.)

Power, Edward, (1959), *Evolution of Educational Doctines,* (New York: Appleton—Century Cofts, Inc.)

Quintilian, (1924), *Instituio Oratoria,* (tr.) Butler H.E. (London: Williams Heinemann).

Robin, Barrow, (1973), *Athenion Democracy,* (London: Macmillan Edu. Ltd.)

Rousseau, J.J., (1938), *Emile* (tr.) Barbara Foxley, (New York: E.P. Dutton & Co. Inc.)

Ruccius, Walter M., (1916), *John Bugenlagen Pomeranus,* (Philadelphia: The United Lutheran Publishing House).

Rousseau, J. J., (1762), *Emile* (tr.) J. M. Dent and sons (1966), (London, Everyman Ed.)

Rusk, Robert, (1969), *Doctrines of the Great Educators,* Fourth Ed. (London: Macmillan)

Sartre, Jean-Paul, (1956), *Being and Northingness: An Essay on Phenomenological Ontology,* (tr.) Hazel Barnes, (New York: Philosophical Library)

Smith, Frank, (1931), *A History of English Education,* (London Universitz of London Press).

Stabart, J. C., (1971), *The Gradeur that was Rome* (London: Sidgwick and Jackson)

Taylor, H.O., (1930), *The Medieval Mind,* (New York: Macmillan Co.)

Thakur, A.S., Emeka, M., Sharma, A.P., (1983), *Great Western Educational Philosphers in African Perspective,* (New Delhi: National Publishing House, Daryaganj)

Weiss, Robert, (1957), *Humanism in England During the Fifteenth Century,* (Oxford: B. Blackwell)

Wilkins, Ernest H., (1961), *Life of Petrarch,* (Chicago: University of Chicago Press)

Woodward, William H., (1904), *Desiderius Erasmus, Concerning the Aim and Method of Education,* (New York: Cambridge University Press)

Woodward, William H., (1924), *Studies in Education During the Age of the Renaissance,* (New York: Cambridge University Press)

Woodruft, Douglas, (1934), *Charlemagne,* (London: P. Davis Ltd.)

INDEX